D0278176

ESSENTIAL
MENORCA

★ Best places to see 34–55   ■ Featured sight

Original text by Tony Kelly
Updated by Jane Egginton

© Automobile Association Developments Limited 2009
First published 2007
Reprinted 2009. Information verified and updated

ISBN: 978-0-7495-6015-7

Published by AA Publishing, a trading name of Automobile Association Developments
Limited, whose registered office is Fanum House, Basing View, Basingstoke,
Hampshire RG21 4EA. Registered number 1878835.

Colour separation: MRM Graphics Ltd
Printed and bound in Italy by Printer Trento S.r.l.

A03616
Maps in this title produced from mapping © KOMPASS GmbH, A-6063
Rum/Innsbruck

About this book

This book is divided into five sections.

The essence of Menorca pages 6–19
Introduction; Features; Food and drink; Short break including the 10 Essentials

Planning pages 20–33
Before you go; Getting there; Getting around; Being there

Best places to see pages 34–55
The unmissable highlights of any visit to Menorca

Best things to do pages 56–77
Places to have lunch by the sea; top activities; family beaches; best viewpoints; places to take the children and more

Exploring pages 78–186
The best places to visit in Menorca, organized by area

Maps
All map references are to the maps on the covers. For example, Maó (Mahón) has the reference ✚ 23K – indicating the grid square in which it is found.

Admission prices
An indication of the cost of admission to attractions is given by € signs:
€ inexpensive (under €3), €€ moderate (€3–€6), €€€ expensive (over €6).

Hotel prices
Price are per room per night: € budget (under €50); €€ moderate (€50–€100); €€€ expensive to luxury (over €100)

Restaurant prices
Price for a three-course meal per person without drinks: € budget (under €15); €€ moderate (€15–€30); €€€ expensive (over €30)

Contents

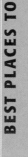

BEST THINGS TO DO

EXPLORING...

56 – 77   78 – 186

The essence of...

Menorca is the quiet one of the Balearics. Mallorca may be larger, Ibiza may be brasher, but Menorca remains calm and dignified, confident of its own charms.

The wild olive trees of the north coast, bent into shape by the *tramuntana* winds, are symbolic of a people and an island shaped by history and a rugged landscape. Numerous invasions have not changed the Menorcan character – courteous and welcoming to strangers, yet self-sufficient and fiercely independent. Tourism has brought many benefits, but the Menorcans have not let themselves get carried away. The impression you get is of an island at ease with itself.

features

'Wind and stones', 'a rock strewn with earth' –
Menorca has been called many things. 'The blue
and white island', for the clarity of its light and the
contrasts between dazzling white houses and a
turquoise sea. 'An open-air museum', for its
megalithic monuments – piles of ancient stones
which blend into the modern landscape.

Romans and Byzantines, British and Spanish
colonists have all left their mark; even the tourist
invasion since the 1960s has created its own
monuments. But the biggest influence on Menorca
remains what it has always been – the sea.

There are plenty of crowded beach resorts,
indistinguishable from their equivalents elsewhere;
yet at the same time you find peaceful coves,
where pine-clad rocks surround arcs of fine sand.
Thanks in part to a lack of island coast road, most of
Menorca's beaches remain secluded spots.

The cities at either end of the island personify
Menorca's contrasts. Georgian Maó (Mahón), the

colonial capital, is a place of civil servants and naval
officers, protected by one of the world's great
harbours. Catalan Ciutadella (Ciudadela), all
aristocratic mansions and Gothic churches, is just
45km (28 miles) away but feels like another world.

Between them is a rural landscape of meadows, cattle and drystone walls, punctuated by market towns and gentle hills.

GEOGRAPHY AND LANDSCAPE

- Menorca is the second largest of the Balearic Islands, a group that includes Mallorca, Ibiza and Formentera.
- It lies 225km (140 miles) southeast of Barcelona, at the eastern extremity of Spain, and measures 53km (33 miles) from east to west and 23km (14 miles) from north to south at its widest point.
- Menorca has 220km (137 miles) of coastline, with more beaches than all the other Balearic Islands put together.
- The highest mountain is Monte Toro (357m/ 1,171ft).
- Menorca has at least 15,000km (9,320 miles) of drystone walls and 1,000 prehistoric monuments.

PEOPLE

- Menorca has a population of 76,000, of whom around 24,000 live in Maó and 23,000 in Ciutadella.

LANGUAGE

Locals speak Menorcan (a dialect of Catalan), as well as Spanish – Castellan. Place names often have a version of each, although signs are not always consistent. Where appropriate, both names have been given in this book, with the Menorcan spelling first and the Castellan following in brackets.

TOURISM

- International tourism began in Menorca in the 1950s and developed quickly. No-frills flights to the island from the UK have increased its accessibility but Menorca remains a relaxing destination, relatively unspoiled by mass tourism.

food & drink

Menorca's cookery is firmly rooted in its history. The Arabs introduced almonds and the Spanish brought peppers from America, while the British imported Friesian cattle, still used in today's dairy industry, but the essential ingredients – garlic, tomatoes and olive oil – remain truly Mediterranean.

SEAFOOD

Menorca's island cuisine relies heavily on the products of the sea. Most notable – and expensive – are spiny lobsters from Fornells, used in the classic soup *caldereta de langosta*. Fresh prawns and mussels are abundant; other fish includes mullet, sole and sea bass. Squid is a speciality, stuffed with its own meat; vegetables such as aubergines and peppers are also frequently filled with seafood. A true paella, from Valencia, consists of saffron rice cooked with meat and fish, but its Menorcan equivalent, *arroz marinera*, is based on seafood. Other rice dishes include *arroz caldoso*, a fish and rice stew.

MEAT DISHES

Meat – which could be beef, veal, pork or lamb – is often served roasted with *salsa de grevi* (gravy), a legacy of the British occupation. Menorcans are proud of their sausages, a by-product of the winter *matança* or slaughter of pigs. The best-known are *sobrasada*, made of minced raw pork with hot peppers, and *botifarró* (blood pudding); others include *carn i xua*, *cuixot* and *salsitxa*. Order a

surtido de fiambres (plate of cold cuts) and you might get all of these, along with cured ham and Mahón cheese.

TAPAS

Tapas include octopus, snails and tripe, but two of the simplest are *tortilla*, a cold potato omelette, and *pa amb oli*, literally bread doused with olive oil and smeared with garlic, but often topped with fresh tomato, ham or cheese. Bakers sell *formatjades* and *empanadillas*, small pies filled with sausage, cheese, tuna or spinach, as well as *bocadillos* (filled rolls).

THE ESSENCE OF MENORCA

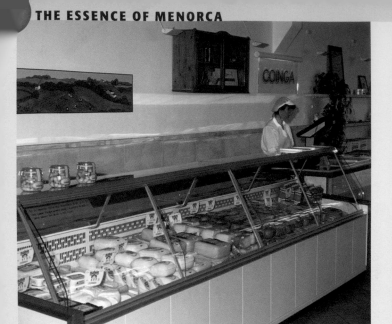

DESSERTS

La Menorquina ice-creams and sorbets, from Alaior, are sold all over Spain. They also produce other frozen desserts. Sweet biscuits are another local speciality, especially *amargas* and *carquinyols* (almond macaroons), while *ensaimadas* are fluffy, spiral pastries often stuffed with fruits and nuts. *Cucusso* is made from honey, raisins and almonds.

CHEESE

Queso Mahón is one of Spain's leading cheeses, with its own *denominación de origen*. Until recently a seasonal farmhouse cheese, it is now produced industrially and exported across the world. Made in square loaves and cured for up to two years, its yellow rind is coated with oil as it matures. Varieties range from *tierno*, eaten mild and young and used to stuff Christmas turkeys, through *semi-curado* and *curado* to the fully mature *añejo*.

DRINKS

There has been something of a revival of Menorcan wine although most of what is consumed on the island is still imported from

mainland Spain. The best reds come from Rioja, made with the *tempranillo* grape and aged in oak. *Cava* is a sparkling wine from Catalunya. Beer is available everywhere – for draught beer, ask for *una caña*. Tap water is generally safe to drink but everyone drinks mineral water – *agua con gas* is sparkling, *sin gas* is still.

GIN

Gin, a spirit flavoured with juniper berries, was already produced in Menorca before the 18th century, but its popularity with British sailors helped to modernize its manufacture. The leading producer is Xoriguer, located on Maó's waterfront, whose gin is sold in characteristic earthenware bottles called *canecas*; they make an attractive souvenir. *Pomada*, gin mixed with lemonade, is a refreshing, traditional apéritif.

short break

If you have only a short time to visit Menorca and would like to take home some unforgettable memories you can do something local and capture the real flavour of the island. The following suggestions will give you a wide range of sights and experiences that won't take very long, won't cost very much and will make your visit very special.

● **Wander the back streets** of Ciutadella (➤ 160–172), where every other house is the palace of a noble family, with hidden architectural details and coats of arms above the door.

● **Go to the trotting races** in Maó or Ciutadella at weekends, the best place to see Menorcans indulge their passion for horses.

● **Seek out** some of Menorca's prehistoric sites and try to unravel the mystery of the *taulas* (T-shaped 'tables' which probably performed some religious ritual function).

● **Take a boat trip** around Maó's deep, natural harbour (➤ 48–49), then stroll along the waterfront for a drink in Cala Figuera (➤ 84).

● **Have lunch by the harbour** at Fornells (➤ 40–41) – *caldereta de langosta* if you can afford it.

● **Walk to a remote beach** that cannot be reached by car – take a picnic and plenty of water, and settle down to your own private view.

● **Find out where** there is a festival going on (➤ 24–25) and drop everything to get there – especially if it is the Festa de Sant Joan in Ciutadella.

● **Make the pilgrimage** – on foot or by car – to Monte Toro (➤ 42–43), the hilltop convent at the centre of the island.

Planning

Before you go

WHEN TO GO

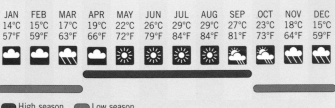

JAN	FEB	MAR	APR	MAY	JUN	JUL	AUG	SEP	OCT	NOV	DEC
14°C	15°C	17°C	19°C	22°C	26°C	29°C	29°C	27°C	23°C	18°C	15°C
57°F	59°F	63°F	66°F	72°F	79°F	84°F	84°F	81°F	73°F	64°F	59°F

High season   Low season

Menorca's climate is typically Mediterranean, and is well known for its mild temperatures. It has an average daily maximum of 20.3°C (68.5°F), rising to 29°C (84°F) in July and falling to 14°C (57°F) in January.

There are approximately 315 days of sunshine a year.

Menorca is the wettest of the Balearic Islands; the rainy season runs from October to April. The average rainfall ranges from approximately 450mm (17in) in the southeast to 650mm (25.5in) in the northeast and the interior.

There are eight distinct winds, of which the fiercest and most common is the *tramuntana*, the cool north wind. The *sirocco* blows from the south, bringing sand from the Sahara in Africa.

WHAT YOU NEED

		UK	Germany	USA	Netherlands	Spain
●	Required					
○	Suggested					
▲	Not required					

Some countries require a passport to remain valid for a minimum period (usually at least six months) beyond the date of entry – contact their consulate or embassy or your travel agent for details.

	UK	Germany	USA	Netherlands	Spain
Passport (or National Identity Card where applicable)	●	●	●	●	▲
Visa (regulations can change – check before you travel)	▲	▲	▲	▲	▲
Onward or Return Ticket	▲	▲	▲	▲	▲
Health Inoculations (tetanus and polio)	▲	▲	▲	▲	▲
Health Documentation (➤ 23, Health Insurance)	●	●	●	●	▲
Travel Insurance	○	○	○	○	○
Driving Licence (national)	●	●	●	●	●
Car Insurance Certificate	●	●	●	●	●
Car Registration Document	●	●	●	●	●

WEBSITES

Spanish Tourist Board:
www.spain.info
www.okspain.org

www.e-menorca.org
www.illesbalears.es

TOURIST OFFICES AT HOME

In the UK

Spanish Tourist Office
✉ PO Box 4009,
London W1A 6NB
☎ 020 7486 8077
www.spain.info

In the USA

Tourist Office of Spain
✉ 666 Fifth Avenue 35th,

New York, NY 10103
☎ 212/265-8822
www.okspain.org

Tourist Office of Spain
✉ 8383 Wilshire Boulevard,
Suite 956, Beverly Hills,
CA 90211
☎ 323/658-7188
www.okspain.org

HEALTH INSURANCE

Nationals of EU and certain other countries can get medical treatment in Spain with the European Health Insurance Card (EHIC), although private medical insurance is still advised and is essential for all other visitors.

Dental treatment is not usually available free of charge. A list of *dentistas* can be found in the yellow pages of the telephone directory. Treatment should be covered by private medical insurance.

TIME DIFFERENCES

GMT
12 noon

Menorca
1PM

Germany
1PM

USA (NY)
7AM

Netherlands
1PM

Spain
1PM

Menorca is one hour ahead of Greenwich Mean Time (GMT+1), but from late March until late September, summer time (GMT+2) operates.

NATIONAL HOLIDAYS

1 January *New Year's Day*
6 January *Epiphany*
March/April *Maundy Thursday, Good Friday and Easter Monday*
1 May *Labour Day*
May/June *Corpus Christi*
25 July *Saint James' Day*
15 August *Assumption of the Virgin*

8 September *Birthday of the Virgin Mary*
12 October *Columbus Day*
1 November *All Saints*
6 December *Constitution Day*
8 December *Immaculate Conception*
25 December *Christmas Day*

26 December *Saint Stephen's Day*

Shops, banks and offices close on these days, but in the main resorts many places remain open. In addition, each town celebrates its own patron saint's day.

WHAT'S ON WHEN

January *Los Reyes Magos* (5 Jan): The Three Kings arrive by boat in Maó (Mahón) to deliver Christmas presents to the city's children the next day. Similar events take place across the island.

Sant Antoni Abad (16–17 Jan): Bonfires, dancing and fancy dress parties in Maó, Es Castell and elsewhere on 16 January; on 17 January, following a Mass in Ciutadella cathedral, there is a horseback procession to Plaça Alfons III.

March/April *Setmana Santa* (Holy Week): Palm branches are blessed in the island's churches on Palm Sunday and taken home to adorn balconies and front doors. Processions in Maó and Ciutadella (Ciudadela) on Good Friday.

June *Sant Joan* (23–24 Jun): This is the most colourful of all Menorca's festivals, with traditions dating back to the Middle Ages. On the evening of 23 June there is a horse-back procession around the Plaça des Born in Ciutadella, and on 24 June there are further processions, a Mass in the cathedral, jousting tournaments and finally a firework display in the Born. Celebrations get under way on the Sunday before 24 June (the Day of the Sheep), when a live lamb is carried around town on the shoulders of a man dressed in sheepskins.

July *La Verge del Carme* (16 Jul): Processions and the blessing of fishing boats in Maó, Ciutadella and Fornells in honour of the protector of fishermen. Held all over the Balearic Islands.
Sant Martí (3rd Sun): Processions of horses, giants and Carnival figures in Es Mercadal.
Sant Jaume (24–26 Jul): Horse-back parades and merriment in Es Castell.
Sant Antoni (4th weekend): Annual festivities in Fornells, including *jaleo* dancing on the waterfront.

July/August *Festival de Música de Maó* Music festival in Maó with concerts in Santa Maria Church and Teatre Principal.

August *Sant Cristòfol* (early Aug): Es Migjorn Gran's annual festival

features a 'blessing of the vehicles' by the parish priest.
Sant Llorenç (second weekend): Dancing and horseback parades in the streets of Alaior.
Sant Bartomeu (23–25 Aug): Frolics in Ferreries, with cavalcades, music and dancing.

September *La Verge del Gràcia* (7–9 Sep): Maó's main festival features cavalcades, street parties, donkey races, firework displays and regattas in the harbour.

December *Nadal* (Christmas Eve and Christmas Day, 24–25 Dec): Midnight Mass is held in churches throughout Menorca.

Getting there

BY AIR

Maó Airport

5km (3 miles) to city centre

🚈 N/A

🚌 15 minutes

🚗 10 minutes

Spain's national airline, Iberia (tel: 971 36 90 15; www.iberia.com), has scheduled flights to Menorca from the Spanish mainland and major European and North American cities, but most visitors arrive by charter or budget airlines. There are buses from the airport into central Maó every 30 minutes daily during the summer, and Monday to Friday in winter; hourly at weekends. For Maó airport information, tel: 971 15 70 00.

INTER-ISLAND FLIGHTS

Iberia operates several flights a day between Mallorca and Menorca (flight time: 30 minutes). There are no direct flights from Menorca to Ibiza (you will be routed via Mallorca). Fares are inexpensive but you must reserve ahead at the height of summer (Iberia domestic flight reservations, tel: 902 40 05 00; www.iberia.com).

BY SEA

Ferries from mainland Spain are run by Acciona Transmediterránea (tel: 902 45 46 45; www.trasmediterranea.es). The company offers a high-speed service to Maó from Valencia and Barcelona. The journey is about 12 hours from Valencia and 8 hours from Barcelona; both trips are overnight.

INTER-ISLAND FERRIES

There are regular ferry services between Menorca and Mallorca. Trasmediterránea (tel: 971 36 60 50) operates a weekly car ferry between Palma and Maó (6 hours). The Maó ferry terminal is only 5 minutes by car to the town centre. There is no bus link. There are also services twice daily, with an extra service on Saturdays from mid-June to September, between Ciutadella and Port d'Alcúdia on Mallorca with Iscomar (tel: 971 43 75 00; www.iscomar.com).

Getting around

PUBLIC TRANSPORT

Buses Menorca has an extensive network of buses linking Maó and Ciutadella with most coastal resorts and interior villages, supplemented by more intermittent local services between smaller towns and resorts. Destinations are marked on the front of the bus. Check the time of the last bus back. A timetable is published daily in the *Diario* newspaper.

INTER-ISLAND FERRIES

For day-trips to Mallorca, Cala Ratjada Tours (tel: 902 10 04 44; www.calaratjadatours.es) have a passenger-only fast catamaran service to Cala Ratjada (45 minutes) that departs several times daily from Ciutadella, making it possible to leave in the morning and return the same day. Baleària (tel: 902 16 01 80; www.balearia.com) also operates fast ferries between Ciutadella and Port d'Alcúdia (1 hour). Details of all these services can be found in the *Diario* newspaper and on the company websites.

TAXIS

Taxis can be hired at ranks (indicated by a blue square with a 'T'), on the street (by flagging down those with a green light) or at hotels. They are good value within Maó but expensive over long distances. A list of tariffs is usually displayed at taxi ranks.

DRIVING

- Drive on the right.
- There are no motorways. The only main road links Maó and Ciutadella (speed limit: 90kph/56mph)
- Speed limit on minor roads: 40kph/25mph
- Speed limit on urban roads: 40kph/25mph
- Seat belts must be worn at all times. Children under 12 must use an approved child seat/harness.
- Random breath-testing takes place. Never drive under the influence of alcohol.
- Rental cars take either unleaded petrol *(sin plomo)* or diesel *(gasoleo)*. There are 24-hour petrol stations in Maó, Ciutadella, Sant Lluís and on the C721 highway at Alaior and Es Mercadal. There are few petrol stations away from the main highway. Most accept credit cards.

- If your own car breaks down and you are a member of an AIT-affiliated motoring club, you can call the Real Automóvil Club de España (tel: 900 11 81 18; www.race.es). If the car is rented, follow the instructions given in the documentation; most of the international rental firms provide a rescue service.
- An international driving licence is required for North American visitors.

CAR RENTAL

The leading international car rental companies have offices at Maó airport and you can rent a car in advance (essential in peak periods) either direct or through a travel agent. Local companies offer competitive rates and will usually deliver a car to the airport.

FARES AND TICKETS

Tickets for tourist attractions can be bought on arrival if travelling independently; discounts for children and families are sometimes offered. Tickets for tours can be purchased at hotel receptions or from travel agents and usually include the cost of any attractions visited.

Some companies offer online discounts for booking, or for tickets bought 48 hours in advance. The island is a popular destination for older travellers and senior citizen discounts are sometimes available.

Being there

TOURIST OFFICES
(Oficinas d'Informació Turística)
Airport (inside arrivals terminal)
☎ 971 15 71 15

Ciutadella
Plaça de la Catedral 5
☎ 971 38 26 93
Fornells
Plaça des Forn
☎ 971 15 84 30
Maó
Plaça S'Esplanada
☎ 971 36 37 90
Port de Ciutadella
Comandància de Marina, Moll Nord
☎ 971 48 09 35
Port de Maó
Moll de Llevant 2
☎ 971 35 59 52

TIPS/GRATUITIES

Yes ✓ No ✗		
Restaurants (if service not included)	✓	10%
Cafés/bars	✓	change
Taxis	✓	10%
Porters	✓	€1–€2/bag
Chambermaids	✓	€1–€2/week
Toilets	✗	

MONEY
The euro (€) is the official currency of Spain. Banknotes are in
denominations of 5, 10, 20, 50, 100, 200 and 500 euros and coins are in
denominations of 1, 2, 5, 10, 20 and 50 cents, and 1 and 2 euros. Euro
traveller's cheques are widely accepted, as are major credit cards.
Credit and debit cards can also be used for withdrawing euro notes from
cashpoint machines. Banks can be found in most towns in Menorca.

POSTAL AND INTERNET SERVICES

Stamps can be bought at post offices throughout the island (in Máo, Carrer Bonaire 15 and Ciutadella, Plaça de Born 9). Stamps are also available from tobacconists and postcard shops.

Most of the larger hotels have Internet access, for which there may be a small charge. Many also have free WiFi if you have your own laptop. Internet cafés, some of which also have WiFi, can be found in the main tourist resorts.

TELEPHONES

Most public telephones accept coins, credit cards and phonecards (*tarjetas teléfonicas*), which can be bought at post offices, news kiosks and *tabacos* (tobacconists).

All telephone numbers in the Balearic Islands have the same code (971), but within Menorca you still need to dial the full 9-figure numbers shown in this guide.

To call Menorca from the UK dial 00 34; from the USA dial 011 34.

Most European mobile phones work well in Menorca.

Emergency telephone numbers

Police: (Policía Nacional) 112 or 091
Fire: (Bomberos) 112

Ambulance: (Ambulància) 112 or 061
In any emergency dial: 112

International dialling codes

From Menorca (Spain) to:
UK: 00 44
Germany: 00 49

USA: 00 1
Netherlands: 00 31

EMBASSIES AND CONSULATES

UK ☎ 971 71 24 45
Germany ☎ 971 36 16 68

USA ☎ 971 40 37 07
France ☎ 971 73 03 01

HEALTH ADVICE

Sun advice The sunniest (and hottest) months are July and August, with an average of 11 hours sun a day and daytime temperatures of 29°C (84°F). Particularly during these months you should avoid the midday sun and use a strong sunblock.

Drugs Prescription and non-prescription drugs and medicines are available from pharmacies *(farmàcias)*, distinguished by a large green cross. They are able to dispense many drugs which would be available only on prescription in other countries.

Safe water Tap water is generally safe, though it can be heavily chlorinated. Mineral water is cheap to buy and is sold as *con gas* (carbonated) and *sin gas* (still). Drink plenty of water during hot weather.

PERSONAL SAFETY

The national police force, the Policía Nacional (brown uniforms) are responsible for law and order in urban areas. Some resorts have their own tourist-friendly Policía Turística. If you need a police station ask for *la comisaría*. To help prevent crime:

- Do not carry more cash than you need.
- Do not leave valuables on the beach or poolside.
- Beware of pickpockets in markets, tourist sights or crowded places.
- Avoid walking alone in dark alleys at night.

ELECTRICITY

The power supply in Menorca is 220–225 volts.

Sockets accept two-round-pin-style plugs, so an adaptor is needed for most non-Continental appliances and a transformer for appliances operating on 100–120 volts.

OPENING HOURS

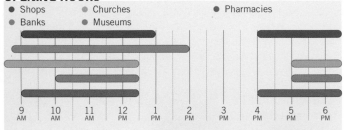

- Shops
- Banks
- Churches
- Museums
- Pharmacies

9 AM · 10 AM · 11 AM · 12 PM · 1 PM · 2 PM · 3 PM · 4 PM · 5 PM · 6 PM

Large department stores, supermarkets and shops in tourist resorts may open outside these times, especially in summer.

In general, pharmacies, banks and shops close on Saturday afternoon, though banks stay open until 4:30pm Monday to Thursday, October to May, but close Saturday, June to September.

The opening times of museums is just a rough guide; some are open longer hours in summer while hours are reduced in winter. Some museums close at weekends and/or Monday.

LANGUAGE

The language that you hear on the streets is most likely to be Menorquín, a version of Catalan (Català), which itself shares features with both French and Spanish but sounds nothing like either and is emphatically a language, not a dialect. Catalan and Spanish both have official status on Menorca, and though Spanish will certainly get you by (it is still the language used by locals to address strangers), it is useful to know some Catalan if only to understand the street signs which are being slowly replaced in Catalan.

yes	*si*	you're welcome	*de res*
no	*no*	how are you?	*com va?*
please	*per favor*	do you speak English?	*parla anglès?*
thank you	*gràcies*		
welcome	*de res*	I don't understand	*no ho entenc*
hello	*hola*		
goodbye	*adéu*	how much?	*quant es?*
good morning	*bon dia*	open	*obert*
good afternoon	*bona tarda*	closed	*tancat*
goodnight	*bona nit*	today	*avui*
excuse me	*perdoni*	tomorrow	*demà*
hotel	*hotel*	room service	*servei d'habitació*
bed and breakfast	*llit i berenar*	bath	*bany*
single room	*habitació senzilla*	shower	*dutxa*
double room	*habitació doble*	toilet	*toaleta*
one person	*una persona*	balcony	*balcó*
one night	*una nit*	key	*clau*
reservation	*reservas*	lift	*ascensor*
café	*cafè*	starter	*primer plat*
pub/bar	*celler*	main course	*segón plat*
breakfast	*berenar*	dessert	*postres*
lunch	*dinar*	bill	*cuenta*
dinner	*sopar*	beer	*cervesa*
table	*mesa*	wine	*vi*
waiter	*cambrer*	water	*aigua*
waitress	*cambrera*	coffee	*café*

Best places to see

1 Barranc d'Algendar (Algendar Gorge)

A dramatic limestone gorge, buzzing with wildlife, which runs for 6km (4 miles) from Ferreries to the south coast.

Menorca's *barrancs*, or gorges, are wild and lonely places, deep clefts formed over tens of thousands of years by the gradual erosion of the limestone plateau in the south.

The gorges attract a huge variety of wildlife, including birds and butterflies. Kestrels and kites nestle among the rushes; you see herons, buzzards and booted eagles. Lizards sun themselves on the rocks and turtles wade through the marshes. The combination of rainfall, humidity and protection from the wind produces a richness of vegetation rarely seen elsewhere.

Algendar Gorge is the most dramatic of all – and one of the most challenging to explore. The stream flows throughout the year, opening out at Cala de Santa Galdana (► 144–145) into a wide river beside the beach. From here it is possible to see the pretty start of the gorge, where pine trees grow out of the cliffs at remarkable angles, but the path is often overgrown and may be blocked.

There is also limited access at the northern end. Take the minor road off the Maó (Mahón) – Ciutadella (Ciudadela) highway 100m (110yds) west of the Cala de Santa Galdana exit; when the tarmac runs out (beside a signed footpath to Ferreries on the old Camí Reial), turn down the lane to your right. You can walk a short way along the gorge before finding your way blocked.

🚶 5E 🍴 At Cala de Santa Galdana (€–€€) 🚌 Buses from Maó, Ciutadella and Ferreries to Cala de Santa Galdana in summer ❓ Conditions underfoot vary greatly from season to season, and you may find locals discourage you from continuing

2 Cala Pregonda

**A peaceful bay, backed by
pine and tamarisk woods, in
a remote and sheltered corner
of the north coast.**

Everyone has their own favourite Menorcan cove
but the one factor they all have in common is that
you cannot reach them by road. Approaching Cala
Pregonda on foot, you wonder what all the fuss is
about – surely a perfect cove cannot have concrete
houses behind the beach? But sit against the dunes
with your back to the houses, surrounded by wild
flowers on a quiet day in spring or autumn, looking
out beyond the shore to the sandstone rocks and
beyond to Cap de Cavallería (➤ 122),

and you begin to feel the magic of this place.

An old Roman road runs from Santa Agueda (➤ 153), but the easiest approach is from Binimel-là (➤ 138). Take the steps over the wall at the west end of Binimel-là beach, follow the track for 10 minutes across salt flats and a pebbly cove, climb a small headland above the dunes, then clamber down to the beach.

The water is crystal-clear, ideal for swimming, though you might have to navigate your way around yachts. A short distance out to sea is a rocky islet with its own sandy beach, just right for a couple of families. Near here is Es Prego, the sandstone outcrop said to resemble a hooded monk (*prego* means proclamation), carved into shape by the fierce north wind. And behind the beach are the pine woods, the best place to take a picnic if you want to escape the crowds – and the sun.

And the houses? They were put up before the restrictions on coastal development were introduced. Even such modest building would not be permitted today.

✚ /B 🍴 None; bring a picnic

3 Fornells

An attractive fishing village of low, whitewashed houses at the edge of a long, sheltered bay.

Fornells is everybody's idea of a Mediterranean fishing village – traditional whitewashed houses around a harbour bobbing with boats, restaurants on the waterfront along a palm-lined promenade. Nowadays, of course, tourism is more important than fishing, but there is still a fishing industry here and the fish in the restaurants is genuinely local and fresh. Fornells is known above all for its spiny lobsters, the essential ingredient in the classic lobster stew *caldereta de langosta*. King Juan Carlos of Spain is said to sail over regularly from Mallorca just to eat lobster at Fornells.

The village is built on the west side of the Bay of Fornells, close to the open sea. The natural harbour is 5km (3 miles) in length, similar to the one at Maó (Mahón). The commander of the first British invasion force to Menorca wrote to his superiors that Maó and Fornells were the two best ports in the Mediterranean.

Founded to defend the north coast against pirate ships, Fornells grew in importance in the 17th century with the building of Castell Sant Antoni, modelled on Fort Sant Felip (➤ 97). The castle ruins stand beside the sea, facing a small island crowned by a watchtower. A promenade from here leads to the cape, where there is a lighthouse, a small rock shrine and another watchtower, **Torre de Fornells.** You can climb to the top of the tower to experience what would once have been the view of approaching invaders.

But most visitors don't go to Fornells for history. They go to soak up its simple beauty, to walk beside the quay or watch the water sports, then choose a harbourside restaurant to enjoy the freshest fish possible.

✚ 9B 🍴 Fish restaurants on the quayside (€€–€€€)
🚌 Buses from Maó (Mahón)

Torre de Fornells
🕓 May–Oct Tue–Sat 11–2, 5–8, Sun 11–2 ✋ Inexpensive

4 Monte Toro

The spiritual and physical high point of Menorca – a hilltop convent right at the centre of the island.

Menorca's highest mountain (357m/1,171ft) is crowned by a convent which has become an important centre of pilgrimage. Its name almost certainly derives from *al-tor*, Arabic for 'highest mountain', despite the local legend about a bull (*toro* in Spanish) who discovered a statue of the Virgin in a cleft in the rock.

Get there by driving or walking the twisting 3km (2-mile) road from Es Mercadal (➤ 123); an alternative approach on foot is to follow the track between two white posts at the entrance to San Carlos farm, 1km (0.5 miles) out of Es Mercadal on the Camí d'en Kane (➤ 171).

The simple courtyard is peaceful and attractive – an old well, an olive tree, a 16th-century stone tower, a low whitewashed refectory. You enter the church through a pretty porch with several arches and dozens of potted plants. Even when you get inside the 17th-century Renaissance church, there is little adornment – a plain white dome, tapestries on the walls and a 1943 altarpiece with a statue of the Virgin with the legendary bull at her feet. This is La Verge del Toro, the chief focus of pilgrimage. Mass is said here at 11am each Sunday and the bishop holds an annual service on 8 May to bless the island's fields.

From the terrace and car park there are sea views on all four sides. Look down from the terrace over neat vegetable and herb gardens, which are tended by the community of nuns who still live on Monte Toro.

✚ 9D ☎ 971 37 50 60 🕒 Daily 7am–8pm (6pm winter) 🎫 Free 🍴 Café and restaurant (€) ❓ 8 May – blessing of the fields, followed by celebrations in Es Mercadal

5 Naveta des Tudons

The oldest roofed building in Spain – a Bronze Age burial chamber aesthetically restored to its former glory.

Of all the prehistoric monuments on Menorca, this is probably the most visited. Until the 1950s it was dishevelled and overgrown; for centuries it had been used as a cattle-shed but was fully restored between 1959 and 1960 and again in 1975.

The word *naveta* describes a burial chamber, built in the shape of an upturned boat. Most are horseshoe-shaped in design, with a low, narrow entrance at the straight end and a small ante-chamber leading into the main burial chamber. Some, like this, were built on two levels; the bodies were left to decompose upstairs and the bones were subsequently transferred to the ground-floor ossuary. Excavations in the 1950s revealed at least 100 corpses in Naveta des Tudons, some with bronze bracelets still around their arm bones.

Navetas are unique to Menorca – of around 45 remaining, this is in the best condition. Although a notice warns you not to disturb the stones by climbing, you can enter the *naveta* on hands and knees for a close look at the main chamber, supported by stone columns.

Because it is on the main road so close to Ciutadella (Ciudadela), Naveta des Tudons attracts a large number of visitors. Come here early in the morning or late in the afternoon to capture some of the atmosphere and history of this place.

➕ 3D ✉ On Maó–Ciutadella road, 4km (2.5 miles) from Ciutadella ⏱ Free access 🍴 None

6 Plaça des Born, Ciutadella

Open-air cafés and elegant 19th-century buildings – one of the finest city squares in Spain.

During the Fascist era this square at the heart of Ciutadella (Ciudadela) was renamed after General Franco, but everyone continued to call it 'es Born'. The word *born* means parade-ground – the square was used for jousting contests in earlier times and

is still the venue for an equestrian parade during the city's annual festivities in June.

At the centre of the square is an obelisk commemorating those citizens of Ciutadella who were killed or abducted into slavery during the Turkish raid of 1558. Much of Ciutadella was destroyed, including the alcázar or governor's palace. The crenellated town hall, with its Moorish-looking row of palms standing guard, was built in the 19th century on the same site. Peep inside to see the panelled ceilings, portraits of local dignitaries and the Gothic chamber on the first floor.

Across the square are two 19th-century palaces, those of the Torre-Saura and Salord families, built symmetrically to either side of Carrer Major del Born. Their neoclassical facades are dominated by Italianate loggias; the ground floors facing the square are given over to gift shops and cafés. Close by is the 19th-century theatre, and the adjoining coffee-house, Cercle Artístic, with harbour views.

➕ 2D (Ciutadella) 🍴 Restaurants and bars in the square (€–€€) 🚌 Buses from west coast resorts to Plaça de S'Esplanada in summer; buses from Maó (Mahón) arrive 5 mins walk away ❓ Festa de Sant Joan 23–24 Jun

7 Port de Maó (Maó Harbour)

The glory of Maó (Mahón) – a deep, natural harbour that has protected the Menorcan capital throughout its history.

When the European powers fought over Menorca in the 18th century, the greatest prize was the harbour at Maó. The world's second-largest natural harbour, 5km (3 miles) long and up to 900m (2,950ft) wide, was wrongly believed to provide an impregnable Mediterranean base.

The best way to see the harbour is on one of the one-hour boat tours that leave from the foot of the harbour steps in summer. The water is deep but it remains incredibly clear and from a glass-bottomed boat you can see the sea bed.

From the water you get the best views of the 18th-century houses lining either side. High on a cliff between Maó and Es Castell (► 96–97, 98–99) is the Hotel del Almirante, a maroon-and-cream Georgian villa that was the home of the British Admiral Collingwood. Facing it on the north shore is Sant Antoni (Golden Farm), where Nelson is said to have stayed in 1799.

Between Maó and the harbour entrance are three islands. The first, Illa del Rei (King's Island), was the first place to be 'liberated' by Alfonso III; when the British built a hospital here, it was known as 'Bloody Island'. Next comes Illa Plana (Flat Island), a former quarantine island. This duty was taken over in 1900 by the largest island, Lazareto, whose high walls were designed to prevent infections from reaching Maó.

South of Lazareto, at the entrance to the harbour, are the ruins of Fort Sant Felip (► 97); to the north is the headland of La Mola, the most easterly point in Spain.

🚩 *Maó 4b* 🍴 Waterfront restaurants at Maó and Es Castell (€€–€€€) 🚌 Buses between Maó and Es Castell 🛥 Boat tours of harbour from Maó and Es Castell, summer

8 S'Albufera d'Es Grau

A protected wetland area close to the east coast that acts as an important refuge for aquatic birds.

There used to be many more areas of wetland around the Menorcan coast, but most were drained for agriculture by the British or reclaimed for tourist *urbanizacións* in the 1960s. Of those that survive, S'Albufera d'Es Grau is the largest and most important. A 70ha (173-acre) lagoon is separated from the sea by a barrier of sand, creating saltwater marshes beside a freshwater lake.

The shores of the lake are a peaceful spot to stroll, with birdwatching hides and a boardwalk trail. In winter there are migrant colonies of ospreys and booted eagles; in spring and autumn the lake attracts waders and wildfowl. Species regularly seen here include cormorants, herons, spoonbills and terns. You may also spot turtles, toads and snakes.

The lake is separated from the beach at Es Grau (► 128–129) by pine woods and dunes. Es Grau is an old-fashioned seaside village, with fishing boats in the harbour and white houses down to the water's edge. The large beach is perfect for children as the water is shallow all the way out to Illa d'en Colom, seen across a channel 400m (1,300ft) out to sea.

In summer you can take boat trips to the island, where there is a choice of sunny or shady beaches. This is the largest of Menorca's offshore islands; there is evidence of early habitation, with Roman ruins and a Byzantine church. The island, home to a protected species of lizard, is now part of the S'Albufera Park, the focus of Menorca's Biosphere Reserve.

🕇 12E 🚯 Free access to national park 🍴 At Es Grau (€–€€) 🚌 Buses from Maó (Mahón) to Es Grau in summer 🚢 Boat trips to Illa d'en Colom and cruises around the Natural Park in summer ☎ 971 35 98 67 ❓ S'Albufera Natural Park reception centre sometimes offers free guided walks ☎ 971 35 63 02

Son Bou

**Son Bou has a long stretch of fine sandy
beach with marshes, caves and an early
Christian church.**

Much of the south coast is made up of small,
indented coves; Son Bou could hardly be more
different. The longest beach on Menorca, it has
almost 3km (2 miles) of pale golden sand, a
sunbather's dream with facilities from beach bars to
waterskiing and windsurfing. The water shelves

gently and swimming is generally safe, but there are occasional dangerous currents so you should look out for the red and green flags. The beach is so long that it rarely gets crowded; it is always possible, especially at the western end, to find your own secluded spot.

At the east end of the beach, beneath two ugly hotels, is one of Menorca's more remarkable ancient monuments – a fifth-century Christian basilica, discovered in 1953. Similar to North African churches of the same period, it has three naves divided by pillars and a huge font, carved from a single stone. When you realize how long it lay hidden beneath the sand you wonder what further treasures are still waiting to be uncovered.

In the cliffs above the basilica are some large prehistoric burial caves, used as summer houses by Menorcan families. Climb up to these caves for the best views over the beach. Above the west end of the beach, separated by marshland, is the purpose-built resort of Sant Jaume Mediterrani. This has everything you could want for a family holiday – pools, shops and discos, plus the popular Club San Jaime (➤ 71) with its water-chutes and labyrinthine maze.

✚ 18J 🍴 Beach bars and restaurants (€–€€) 🚌 Buses from Maó (Mahón) to Son Bou and Club San Jaime in summer, and shuttle 'train' connecting hotels to the beach

10 Torre d'en Gaumés

An atmospheric abandoned village with impressive Bronze Age monuments and views over the south coast.

The extensive prehistoric settlement of Torre d'en Gaumés contains several well-preserved Talaiotic buildings. Most of it dates from around 1400BC, though there is an even older sepulchre nearby and evidence of habitation until Roman and perhaps medieval times.

Get there by following the signs from the Alaior–Son Bou road. As soon as you leave this road, the three *talaiots* are visible in the distance, 2km (1.2 miles) away down a country lane. A paved road leads around the site, making this the one prehistoric site in Menorca that is accessible to wheelchairs and pushchairs, though the path is bumpy in places and there is no access to the *taula* precinct.

Besides the three *talaiots*, there is a *taula* whose

horizontal stone has collapsed, enabling you to appreciate its design, with a carefully hollowed-out centre to fit on top of the vertical stone. (It is possible that the hollow was enlarged at a later date for

use as a Roman sarcophagus.) Nearby is the best-preserved example of a hypostyle chamber, a roofed building with columns, possibly used as a dwelling, but more likely as a sheep shelter or grain store. There is also an ingenious water storage and filtration system, probably of Roman origin, with channels dug into the rock beneath a large flat surface.

This is a peaceful spot, with wild flowers growing among the ruins and views stretching from Monte Toro (➤ 42–43) to the south coast.

🕂 19J ⚫ May–Sep Tue–Sat 10–8, Sun–Mon 10–2:30; winter free, open access ✋ Inexpensive 🍴 None

Best things to do

Places to have lunch by the sea

Café Balear (€€€)

Taste the fresh fish and seafood beside the harbour. Excellent.
✉ Passeig de Sant Joan 15, Ciutadella (Ciudadela) ☎ 971 38 00 05

Cap Roig (€€)

Fresh fish and sea views on a headland north of Maó (Mahón). Try the grilled sardines or giant clams.
✉ Cala Mesquida ☎ 971 18 83 83

El Mirador (€€–€€€)

A lovely setting on a terrace overlooking the sea, perfectly placed in the 'queen of coves'.
✉ Cala de Santa Galdana ☎ 971 15 45 03

En Caragol (€€)

Seafood, steaks and burgers on a summer terrace overlooking the rocky coves on the road between Bianiancolla and Cala Torret.
✉ Marina de Torret, San Telmo
☎ 629 16 50 89

Es Pla (€€€)

On the edge of the waterfront at Fornells you will find the legendary Es Pla restaurant. It is where the king comes to eat *caldereta de langosta* (spiny lobster stew). It also serves a

delicious *paella* (minimum of two people).

✉ Passeig Es Pla, Fornells

☎ 971 37 66 55

La Minerva (€€€)

A waterfront restaurant in an old flour mill, with a jaunty nautical theme and a floating extension in the port.

✉ Moll de Levant, Maó

☎ 971 35 19 95

Sirocco (€€)

Sirocco serves tasty seafood dishes in a converted cave beside the harbour. Good-value *menú del día*.

✉ Moll de Cales Fonts 39, Es Castell

☎ 971 36 79 65

Susy (€)

This summer bar and restaurant, on one of Menorca's most beautiful beaches, is considered by some to be *the* perfect spot on the island.

✉ Cala Macarella ☎ 971 35 94 67

Tamarindos (€€)

Fresh fish and harbourside views with tables on a wooden jetty by the water's edge.

✉ Es Grau ☎ 971 35 94 20

Best walks

A coastal circuit of the island
The Camí de Cavalls is a historic 170km (105-mile) bridle path that circles the island. The whole coast can be walked, apart from two built-up sections in the east and west. It takes about a week to complete on foot, but it is also possible to do it on horseback or bicycle. If you are not energetic enough to contemplate the whole circuit, consider a section of the coast nearest to where you are staying.

Around the historic town of Ciutadella (▶ 166–167)
Take in the main squares and sights such as the cathedral and the Bishop's Palace as well as two museums – the Museu del Pintor Torrent and Museu Municipal, with an option of a stroll along the seafront.

A coastal walk from Es Grau to Sa Torreta (▶ 128–129)
Enjoy a cliff-top footpath with sea and beach views, passing a lagoon, rural farmland and pine woods.

An inland route near Ferreries (▶ 150–151)
Walk into a valley with views of a dramatic limestone gorge, and through fields to a prehistoric village.

A stroll through the town of Es Castell (▶ 98–99)
Begin at the town square to visit a military museum and Fort Marlborough, walking around a bay and into a little beach cove.

Explore Maó (Mahón) – a port walk with a little bit of history (▶ 88–89)
Discover pretty squares and harbour views, taking in the Museu de Menorca and some atmospheric alleyways.

Top activities

● Beach activities – most of the larger beaches rent out equipment. Pedaloes (pedal-boats) are ideal for the whole family to enjoy. Canoes, kayaks, jet-skis and giant inflatables are available at some beaches.

● Birdwatching – the best sites are the S'Albufera marshes, the southern gorges and the wilder coastal areas.

● Caving – the coast of Menorca is littered with caves, some used as ancient burial sites, others as dwellings in the Bronze and Iron ages. The best known are at Cala Morell (► 175). Some are still occupied today, such as those at Cales Coves (► 120–121) and Son Bou (► 52–53).

● Cycling – bicycles can be hired in most parts of the island to explore both the coast and inland. A number of cycle routes have recently been opened up, including Camí de Cavalls (► 60–61).

● Diving – the clear waters in many of Menorca's bays make for excellent diving. Remember, it can be dangerous to fly less than 24 hours after diving.

● Golf – there's only one course, but you can get a good game and spend a pleasant day at the Club Son Parc (► 130–131).

● Horseback riding – you can hire horses and ponies in Alaior, Sant Climent, Ciutadella and Maó.

● Sailing – the calm waters around Menorca are perfect for sailing; there are no tides, few currents and the only real hazard is the *tramuntana* wind.

● Walking – one of the best pursuits on the island, with countryside, hill, coastal and some wonderful winter walking opportunities available. Always take plenty of water, some food and use sun protection.

● Wind- and kite-surfing – boards and equipment can be rented at several of the larger beach resorts in summer. Tuition is sometimes available as well.

Family beaches

BEST THINGS TO DO

- Cala de Santa Galdana (➤ 144–145)
- Es Grau (➤ 50, 128–129)
- Sant Tomàs (➤ 152–153)
- Son Bou (➤ 52–53)
- Son Parc (➤ 130–131)

Remote beaches and quiet coves

Arenal de Son Saura – whether you go by car or you walk this isn't the easiest place to reach but it's well worth the effort. A little taste of paradise (➤ 173).

Cala d'Algaiarens (also known as La Vall) – located in the north and nestling among the Menorcan pines; don't be put off by the private signs. You will have to pay for parking in the summer. Avoid weekends in high season if you want real peace and quiet (➤ 139).

Cala del Pilar – with the effort it takes to get to this wild, out-of-the-way spot, you'd think it would always be quiet, but it does attract locals at the weekends. (➤ 140).

Cala en Turqueta – a lovely cove, a sheltered horseshoe of white sand sloping gently into the sea providing an idlyllic retreat (➤ 140).

Cala Escorxada – certainly one of the harder coves to get to; probably the best response to landowner restrictions is to visit by boat (➤ 141).

Calas Macarella and Macarelleta – the lovely cove of Cala Macarella (➤ 142–143) still manages to get crowded, so the more adventurous can

cross the headland or swim to find privacy at Cala Macarelleta with its picture-postcard beach.

Cala Mitjana – best reached on foot from Cala de Santa Galdana (➤ 143), this cove is down a small rocky track off the road from Ferreries to Galdana. After about 30 minutes you will find the rocky cove of Mitjana and the delightful south-facing sandy beach bounded by wooded cliffs full of caves.

Cala Pregonda – there are some houses here, but it is still a remote and essentially quiet place (➤ 38–39), great for swimming and for the spectacular path that connects with Cap de Cavallería (➤ 122).

Cala Trebalúger – with only pedestrian or maritime access, this popular anchorage for boats is hard to get to, but you will be rewarded for your effort (➤ 146).

Cales Coves – you can't beat your first sighting of the coves, with more than 100 prehistoric caves carved out of the rock, but it will take you a bit of a hike or a rough drive to get there (➤ 120–121). The beach sometimes suffers from seaweed washed up from the sea.

Best viewpoints

- Cala Macarella/Cala Macarelleta – the headland (➤ 142–143)

- Cales Coves (➤ 120–121)

- Cap de Cavallería (➤ 122)

- Cap de Favàritx (➤ 122–123)

- Castell Sant Nicolau, Ciutadella (at sunset) (➤ 160)

- Cova d'en Xoroi, Cala en Porter (➤ 119)

- Mirador de Sa Punta, Cala de Santa Galdana (➤ 144–145)

- Monte Toro (➤ 42–43)

- Santa Agueda (➤ 153)

- Son Mercer de Baix, Ferreries (➤ 149)

Places to take the children

CALA EN BLANES
Aquapark
This waterpark near Ciutadella has waterslides, trampolines, pools, bouncy castles, playgrounds, video games, go-karts and a pizzeria.

✉ Avinguda de los Delfines ☎ 971 38 87 05; www.aquacenter-menorca.com

🕐 May–Oct daily 10:30–6:30

CALA EN BOSC
Aquarock
Thrills and spills including the Kamikaze waterslide plus swimming pools, wave machines and go-karting.

✉ Cala en Bosc ☎ 971 387822; www.aquarockmenorca.com 🕐 May–Oct daily 10:30–6

FERRERIES
Club Escola Menorquina
The equestrian show here features carriage rides, dressage displays and performances of prancing and rearing horses. Children can go for a ride in a donkey-cart during the interval.

✉ Carretera Cala Galdana, km 0.5 ☎ 971 37 34 97; www.showmenorca.com

🕐 Jun–Sep Wed, Sun 8:30pm

Son Martorellet
Elegant displays of horse-riding and equestrian ballet. Miniature train ride for kids.

✉ Carretera Cala Galdana, km I.5 ☎ 609 04 94 93; www.sonmartorellet.com

🕐 May–Oct Tue, Thu 8:30pm

MAÓ (MAHÓN)
Lloc de Menorca
Typical Menorcan farm with animals and local produce where children can learn about island agriculture and feed the goats.

✉ Carretera Maó–Alaior, km 7 ☎ 971 37 24 03; www.llocdemenorca.com

🕐 Daily 10–4

Parc d'es Freginal

A pine-filled park, with gardens, fountains, ponds and swings, in the centre of town. There is also a children's playground on nearby Plaça de S'Esplanada.

✉ Entrance on Costa d'en Deià
🕐 Daily 8–8

Yellow Catamarans

Daily sailings on a glass-bottom boat that comes close to a 'Yellow Submarine' experience.

✉ Moll de Llevant, 12 ☎ 639 67 63 51; www.yellowcatamarans.com

SON BOU
Club San Jaime

A wealth of activities to keep little ones amused, including a swimming pool, a water-chute and a remarkable interlocking wooden maze. The whole complex is arranged around landscaped gardens with views over the marshes and out to sea.

✉ Sant Jaume Mediterrani ☎ 971 37 27 87 🕐 May–Oct daily 10–7

SON PARC
Hort de Llucaitx Park

Countryside recreation centre with a wide range of activities for kids of all ages – pony-trekking, bike rental, cart rides, playgrounds and mini-golf, plus farm animals to feed.

✉ Carretera Maó–Fornells, km 17 ☎ 971 18 86 07 🕐 May–Oct daily 10–8; Sat–Sun only in winter

a drive

around the southeast

This drive takes in Menorca's only stretch of coast road.

Start in Maó (Mahón), leaving Plaça de S'Esplanada along Avenida Josep Anselm Clavé, passing the football stadium and following signs to Sant Lluís. Go through Sant Lluís (➤ 100–101) and over the roundabout (traffic circle) towards the coast. After 1km (0.5 miles) , take the right fork to Punta Prima and after another 1km (0.5 miles) – when you see a satellite mast ahead – fork left, climbing a hill and dropping down to the sea. As you enter Punta Prima (➤ 100), a right turn at the first roundabout takes you on to the coast road.

Follow this road for 4km (2.5 miles), passing rocky coves and the small resort of Cala Torret before reaching Binibèquer beach. Another 1km (0.5 miles) takes you to Binibeca (Binibèquer) Vell (➤ 92). After the village, turn right, left and left again at the next roundabout to bypass Binibeca Vell and return to the sea. As the road runs out, turn inland – go left at the T-junction and swing wide left at the three-way intersection to return to the coast.

Eventually the road turns inland across a rocky landscape, then gentle countryside on its way to Sant Climent (➤ 100).

Turn left through the village on to the Cala en Porter road; after 4km (2.5 miles), just past the turn-off to Cales Coves, take the country road to Alaior on your right.

You cross a typical landscape of meadows and drystone walls, as well as passing some interesting prehistoric sites.

On reaching Alaior (➤ 116), turn right and return to Maó on the main road.

Distance 48km (30 miles)
Time 2 hours plus lunch
Start/end point Maó ✚ 23J
Lunch Los Bucaneros (€€) ✉ Binibèquer beach ☎ No telephone
📅 May–Oct only

73

Art galleries

MAÓ (MAHÓN)
Galería Artara
Lovely gallery with exhibitions of Menorcan artists.
✉ Calle Rosario 18 ☎ 971 35 29 12; www.galeriaartara.com

Sala de Cultura La Caixa
A gallery in the heart of the pedestrian shopping quarter hosting temporary exhibitions of modern art.
✉ Carrer Nou 25 ☎ 971 35 30 62

Sala de Cultura Sa Nostra
Art exhibitions in the former convent of Sant Antoni.
✉ S'Arraval 32 ☎ 971 36 68 54

CIUTADELLA (CIUDADELA)
Museu del Pintor Torrent
Collection of works by José Torrent (➤ 165).
✉ Carrer Rafel 11 ☎ 971 38 04 82

Sala de Cultura Sa Nostra
Exhibition rooms and educational activities aimed at the cultural and social development of the Balearic Islands.
✉ Carrer Santa Clara 9 ☎ 971 48 06 86

ES MERCADAL
Galeria del Sol
Exhibitions of work by local and international artists.
✉ Via Ronda 28 ☎ 971 15 40 07

ES MIGJORN GRAN
Galeria Migjorn Gran
Exhibitions of work by the British watercolour artist Graham Byfield and other local artists at this English-run gallery.
✉ Carrer Sant Llorenc 12 ☎ 971 37 03 64 🕔 May–Sep Mon–Fri 10–1

Archaeological sites

Cala Morell – this is one of the easiest and best places to view the late Bronze Age and early Iron Age caves (➤ 175).

Cales Coves – not as accessible as the caves at Cala Morell, but certainly remarkable, there are more than 100 prehistoric caves here. You may only get the chance to look from the outside (➤ 120–121).

Naveta des Tudons – the best known of the burial monuments from the pre-Talaiotic period at the beginning of the Bronze Age when the first human presence has been verified on Menorca (➤ 44–45).

Sant Agustí Vell – although a more minor site, it contains the only surviving *talaiot* of its type on the island (➤ 152).

Son Bou – here you will find an intersting early Christian basilica left behind from the end of the Roman era dating from the 5th century (➤ 52–53).

Son Catlar – this is the largest of Menorca's prehistoric sites. There is a massive stone wall, a *taula* compound and *talaiots* here as well (➤ 179).

Torelló – this spot is especially interesting as it features an ancient *talaoit* and a 6th-century basilica all within a stone's throw of the airport (➤ 102–103).

Torralba d'en Salort – here you will find the remains of a complete village, with a *taula*, a *talaiot* and a well that is 46m (150ft) deep, with nine flights of steps and a stone handrail hewn out of the rock (➤ 131).

Torre d'en Gaumés – this is the largest prehistoric village to be found in the Balearic Islands. It is one of the sites founded during the great expansion around 1400BC and features a *taula*, a T-shaped standing stone believed to be a single monument of worship (➤ 54–55).

Trepucó – on the outskirts of Maó (Mahón), this site is some 3,000 years old and is dominated by a massive *taula*, the tallest on the island, and a huge *talaiot* (➤ 103).

Exploring

Menorca has long lived in the shadow of its Balearic neighbours, the bigger Mallorca and the brasher Ibiza, but it remains aloof, quietly confident of its own charms. It actually has more beaches than Mallorca and Ibiza combined but they are often harder to find. Not that Menorca is all about beaches, it boasts a plethora of ancient sites and monuments, many still lying undisturbed. Its two major towns – Maó (Mahón) and Ciutadella (Ciudadela) – are strikingly different, yet both pretty and historic and worth a visit. Away from the towns and beaches is a rural landscape and a handful of market towns where life is relatively unchanged. As a UNESCO Biosphere Reserve, Menorca is assured of a future protected from mass development, where traditional industries and tourism work in partnership at conserving the natural beauty of a lovely, if sometimes underrated, island.

Maó and the Southeast

You cannot separate Maó from its harbour – it is the reason for its very existence. It is why the great powers fought over Menorca for so long and why the British moved the capital from Ciutadella to Maó in 1722.

Maó
(Mahón)

The best way to arrive is by boat, watching as the city appears, a jumble of attractive, whitewashed houses which seem to grow out of the old sea walls. Ferries from Barcelona, cruise ships and naval vessels, luxury yachts and even the odd fishing boat, share space in the deep, clear waters and the narrow waterfront road is lined with restaurants and bars.

The area beyond Maó to the south coast, where the British first landed in 1708, has a strong sense of history, and in places there is a colonial feel, especially noticeable in the Georgian town of Es Castell.

MAÓ (MAHÓN)

There was a city here in Roman times; its name, Magón, may be that of Hannibal's brother but is more likely derived from a Phoenician word meaning 'shelter'. Modern Maó (which is frequently still referred to by its Spanish name, Mahón) dates from the Catalan conquest; it was Alfonso III, the conqueror, who began both the Church of Santa Maria and the city walls, of which only the gateway of Pont de Sant Roc survives.

The greatest influence on the city you see today, though, is probably British. They moved the capital to Maó and filled it with Georgian-style architecture. Streets such as Carrer Isabel II are adorned with grand 18th-century houses, with furniture in the style of Sheraton and Chippendale.

For three centuries Maó has had to serve its foreign rulers, whether British, French or Spanish. The result is a city that is serious rather than stylish, industrious rather than flamboyant. At times its status as a capital makes it feel like a much bigger city; at other times, when work is done for the day and everyone greets everyone else by name during the evening *passeig* across the Plaça de S'Esplanada, it feels like little more than a small village.
✚ 23K

Ajuntament (Ayuntamiento)

Mao's town hall was built in 1613 but completely refashioned in 1788 with the addition of an English clock, a gift from the first British governor, Sir Richard Kane. A stone stairway leads to the portico, where plaques record the completion of the original building, together with royal visits and coronations. Also here is a sculpted image of Saint Sebastian, patron saint of Maó. The lobby is lined with portraits of former governors, including the Count of Lannion (the first French governor) and the Count of Cifuentes, the first Spanish governor following British rule. A watercolour by the Italian painter Giuseppe Chiesa shows French troops attacking Fort Sant Felip in 1756. Near here is the municipal debating chamber,

with velvet armchairs for the deputies, wooden benches for the public and a gallery of portraits of 'illustrious Menorcans'.

✚ *Maó 3c* ✉ Plaça Constitució ☎ 971 36 98 00 🕐 During office hours ✋ Free 🍴 Nearby in Plaça Bastió (€–€€)

Ateneu

For a city with the population of a small provincial town, Maó has a rich intellectual tradition, perhaps a result of the exposure to so many foreign cultures and ideas. The real focus of Mao's intellectual life is this scientific, literary and artistic association, founded in 1905 and kept open by devoted scholars. Visitors are welcome to see the collections of maps, ceramics, watercolours and fossils.

✚ *Maó 2c* ✉ Sa Rovellada de Dalt 25 ☎ 971 36 05 53; www.ateneumao.org ⊕ Mon–Sat 10–2, 4–10
✋ Free 🍴 In Plaça de S'Esplanada (€–€€)

Cala Figuera

Take the long stairway which leads from Plaça d'Espanya down to the harbour, turn right by the ferry station along Moll de Llevant, follow the seafront promenade and in half an hour, as the road bends to the right, you enter the deep cove of Cala Figuera. This is the fashionable area of Maó – the yacht club is here, along with the casino and the city's top hotel perched up on the cliff. Boathouses, shipyards and fishermen's caves have been turned into shops and bars, and restaurants specializing in everything from sushi to pizza and fresh fish. From here you have a perfect view of the Illa del Rei in the middle of Maó harbour. Cala Figuera was known as 'the English creek' in the days when Royal Navy ships moored here for fresh water. Keep walking around the inlet beyond the restaurants and bars and eventually you reach Cala Fonduco, a peaceful cove just a short distance from the bustle and buzz of the port.

✚ *Maó 8d* 🍴 Waterfront restaurants (€€–€€€)

Collecció Hernández Mora

Joan Hernández Mora (1902–84) was a local historian, author and teacher who devoted much of his spare time to collecting historic documents and artefacts in order to preserve his beloved Menorcan heritage. When he died childless, he left his collection to the city of Maó and it has been turned into this small museum in Plaça Claustre del Carme. The chief part of the display comprises furniture and books; there is also a fascinating collection of maps.

🕂 *Maó 4c* ✉ Plaça Claustre del Carme 5 ☎ 971 35 05 97 ◷ Mon–Sat 10–1 👆 Free 🍴 In nearby Plaça de S'Esplanada (€–€€)

Església del Carme

This massive baroque church was built in 1751 as a Carmelite convent but extensive damage during the Spanish Civil War means that most of what you see is heavily restored. The stern facade leads to a bright interior with bare stone walls and arches and a vaulted ceiling. During the original building of the church, a Roman necropolis was discovered in the vaults, along with various coins and urns which are now in the Museu de Menorca (➤ opposite).

Next to the church, the cloisters of the convent have been turned into a covered shopping mall that incorporates Maó's main market, as well as a supermarket in the basement. This is a good place to buy Mahón cheese, cured hams and local sausages.

✚ *Maó 4c* ✉ Plaça Claustre del Carme ☎ 971 36 24 02 ✋ Free 🍴 In nearby Plaça de S'Esplanada (€–€€)

Museu de Menorca

Come here after exploring Menorca's archaeological sites to discover what happened to all the finds and to piece together the missing links in your knowledge of Menorcan history.

Coins, pottery and funerary objects from several different cultures are gathered under one roof, together with the island's largest collection of fine arts. Among the objects on display is a complete skeleton of *Myotragus balearicus*, a goat-like mammal that once lived on Menorca, but became extinct with the arrival of man. There are Talaiotic sculptures, Roman mosaics and the British coat of arms from Fort Sant Felip (➤ 97).

The setting, in the cloisters of the old Franciscan monastery, is a delight, with galleries arranged around a shady courtyard with an old well at its centre.

✚ *Maó 2b* ✉ Plaça des Monastir ☎ 971 35 09 55 ⏱ Apr–Oct Tue–Sat 10–2, 6–8:30, Sun 10–2; Nov–Mar Mon–Fri 9:30–2, Sat, Sun 10–2 💷 Inexpensive (free on Sat pm and Sun am) 🍴 Nearby in Plaça Bastió (€–€€)

a walk around Maó

Begin in Plaça de S'Esplanada (▶ 90) with your back to the barracks and take Carrer de Ses Moreres in the right-hand corner. Head down this street, noting the bust of Dr Mateu Orfila, known as the founder of modern forensic science, outside No 13.

Continue into Costa de La Plaça, which drops sharply to Plaça Constitució. Turn right into Carrer Nou; this brings you to Plaça Reial. Turn left to reach Plaça Carme. Cross this square diagonally to look into the cloistered market, then head down the steps to the fish market in Plaça d'Espanya.

You could drop down to the waterfront here – but to continue your city walk, follow the stone railings around the square into Plaça Conquesta, with its statue of the Conqueror, Alfonso III. The narrow alley off the square to the right gives a splendid view of the harbour.

Leave Plaça Conquesta diagonally opposite where you entered to return to Plaça Constitució. Turn right by the town hall then bear left into Carrer Isabel II, whose Georgian houses back on to the harbour walls.

The road ends at the Museu de Menorca (▶ 87).

Turn left to enter a maze of narrow streets and whitewashed houses. Another left turn, then right, brings you to Carrer Sant Antoni, emerging beside an old convent, now an art gallery. Turn left to reach Pont de Sant Roc, the only remaining section of the city walls. Turn right into Plaça Bastió and cross this square to enter Carrer d'Alaior. Turn right at the end to return to Plaça de S'Esplanada.

Distance 3km (2 miles)
Time 1 hour
Start/end point Plaça de S'Esplanada ✚ Maó 1d 🚌 Buses from all over the island terminate here
Lunch Café Mirador (€) ✉ Plaça Espanya 2 ☎ 971 35 21 07

Plaça de S'Esplanada

This esplanade – the square between the barracks and the streets of the old town – is the best place to go to see the people of Maó at play. There are pigeons and palm trees, fountains and flower beds, a bowling alley and a children's playground which is busy from late afternoon until dusk. Old men sit in the shade reading newspapers; teenagers queue for popcorn and ice cream.

On Sundays, street entertainers join the crowds. During Maó's festivals Plaça de S'Esplanada acts as an outdoor venue for concerts and parties. The square is lined with cafés – a good place to come during the evening *passeig* to sit with a drink, feeling the pulse of Maó.

🔂 *Maó 1d* 🍴 Restaurants and cafés in the square (€–€€) 🚌 Buses to Maó from across the island terminate here ❓ Market Tue, Sat

Port de Maó

Best places to see, ➤ 48–49.

Santa Maria

Maó's main church was begun soon after the Catalan conquest, then rebuilt in neoclassical style in the 18th century in a gesture of defiance to the island's British, Protestant rulers. Everything here is done on a massive scale. A huge, forbidding facade, broken only by the incongruous presence of four sash windows, leads through the entrance portal to a long, single nave. Most people come to see (or hear) the organ, imported from Barcelona during the Napoleonic Wars with the help of the British. During the summer there are daily concerts of organ music.

✚ Maó 3c ✉ Plaça Constitució ☎ 971 36 39 49 ✋ Free (organ concerts – moderate) 🍴 Nearby in Plaça Bastió (€–€€)

Teatre Principal

When the Greek community was forced out of Maó in the late 18th century, the former Orthodox church was converted into a dance hall; when that outgrew its usefulness, this theatre was built instead. Designed by a Florentine architect, it was the first opera house in Spain when it opened in 1829.

✚ Maó 3c ✉ Costa d'en Deià 46 ☎ 971 35 57 76 🍴 In Plaça Reial (€)

Xoriguer

Menorca's leading gin distillery promotes itself as a tourist attraction in order to entice customers in. In practice all you get to see is the shop, with a few copper stills bubbling away behind glass. You can drink as much as you like – not just gin, but herbal liqueurs ranging from camomile to carob – but without ice or mixers. Another speciality is *calent*, made with aniseed, cinnamon and saffron and served warm to clients 'on the house' by bar owners in Ciutadella each Christmas.

✚ Maó 2b ✉ Moll de Ponent 93 ☎ 971 36 21 97 🕐 Jun–Aug Mon–Fri 8–7, Sat 9–1; Sep–May Mon–Fri 9–1, 4–7 ✋ Free 🍴 On the waterfront (€€–€€€)

More to see in the Southeast

BINIBECA (BINIBÈQUER) VELL

You'll either love or hate this place – to some it is an example of tasteful tourist develop-ment, based on architectural beauty and local style; to others it is tacky, artificial and ugly. One of the earliest coastal developments in Menorca, it was designed to resemble a Mediterranean fishing village, with whitewashed houses, orange trees and sun-drenched patios filled with geraniums. A maze of narrow alleys, Moorish archways, boats and sea views, it would be stunning if only it were authentic. The first giveaway is the name – would a real fishing village be called *Poblat de Pescadors* (Fishing Village)? Then there are the notices for 'reception' and 'public relations', and the signs asking people to be quiet. Look beneath the steeple for the church and you find an alcove with a crucifix – the architect needed a church for the postcards.

You could easily spend your whole holiday here – there is a supermarket, souvenir shops, restaurants and bars, swimming pools, squash courts, a children's play area and a car rental office in case you should want to see Menorca.

The nearest beach is 1km (0.5 miles) away at Binibèquer – here you can rent sunshades, loungers and pedal boats and have lunch at a simple wooden shack which claims to be the only place in Menorca where you can enjoy a drink with your feet in the sea.

✚ 22L 🍴 Several bars and restaurants (€€) 🚌 Buses from Maó (Mahón) in summer

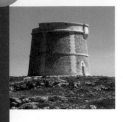

CALA D'ALCAUFAR

This small creek, 4km (2.5 miles) southeast of Sant Lluís, is classically Menorcan – fishermen's cottages reach down to the water and the narrow, curving, sheltered inlet is lined with boats, backed by a sandy beach. This was the site of Menorca's first tourist hotel and it is still a popular weekend trip for the people of Sant Lluís. From the beach you can easily climb on to the cliffs, where a short walk leads to a headland crowned by a Martello tower – beneath which are two grottoes that can be entered by boat.

Cala d'Alcaufar was the site of the first British landing on Menorca, in 1708. Just to the north is S'Algar, reached by a separate road or on a section of the restored coastal bridleway, Camí de Cavalls. The development here is a lot less restrained and the slopes leading down to the sea are a jumble of villas and apartments.

✚ 23L 🍴 Bar/restaurant beside the beach (€) 🚌 Buses from Maó (Mahón) in summer

CALA DE SANT ESTEVE

St Stephen's Creek is named after an early Christian martyr whose remains were said to have been buried here. A deep, narrow inlet at the mouth of Maó harbour, it is mainly notable for its two military fortifications. On one side are the ruins of Fort Sant Felip (➤ 97); on the other, reached by a tunnel, the seven-sided **Fort Marlborough,** built by the British in the late 18th century. Unlike Fort Sant Felip, Fort Marlborough was never destroyed; it has been renovated and opened as a museum. This is great fun and the special effects include explosions in the underground tunnels. You can climb up to the rooftop for more peaceful views.

✚ 24K 🍴 None

Fort Marlborough

☎ 971 36 04 62 🕐 Apr–Dec Tue–Sat 10–1, 5–8, Sun 10–1 ♿ Moderate (free Sun)

CALA MESQUIDA

Despite its proximity to Maó, this remains a peaceful and romantic spot. The capital's citizens come here at weekends, mainly to eat fish at the Cap Roig restaurant, on a slate headland carpeted with wild flowers. At the far end of the village is a wide beach of dark sand protected by cliffs to either side, one of which is dominated by an old watchtower. This was the site of the Duc de Crillon's landing with a Franco-Spanish invasion force in 1781. There is very little modern development (though this was one of Menorca's earliest beach resorts in the 19th century) and the village feels much more remote than it is – and more Menorcan than touristy.

 23J 🍴 Cap Roig (➤ 58)

ES CASTELL

Founded by the British during their second occupation, and originally named Georgetown after George III, Es Castell retains the feel of a British colonial town. The Spanish renamed it Villacarlos after their own king; locals call it Es Castell because of its proximity to Fort Sant Felip (► opposite). The Plaça de S'Esplanada is the former British parade ground, lined with solid Georgian buildings with sash windows and fanlights. Opposite the plum-red town hall, with its British clock tower, is the **Military Museum,** based in the old Cala Corb barracks. It has a collection of flags, guns and maps as well as model reconstructions of Fort Sant Felip and some fine 18th-century English furniture.

Es Castell is the most easterly town in Spain and thus the first to get the morning sun. Cales Fonts, a short walk from the main square, is an attractive sheltered harbour where you can dine at one of the many waterfront restaurants or pick up a boat tour of Port de Maó (► 48–49).

🚌 23K 🍴 Waterfront restaurants in Cales Fonts (€€) 🚍 Buses from Maó (Mahón) ❓ Market Mon and Wed; Festa de Sant Jaume 24–26 Jul

Military Museum
✉ Plaça de S'Esplanada 19 🕐 Jun–Oct Mon–Fri 11–1; Nov–May Mon, Wed, Thu 11–1 ✋ Inexpensive

FORT SANT FELIP

Not much remains of this once impregnable fortress built at the southern entrance to Maó harbour following Turkish raids in the 16th century. It was strengthened by the British and systematically destroyed by the Spanish when they retook Menorca in 1782. On occasional guided tours, you can clamber over the ruins and walk through the underground galleries, where British troops were holed up for six months during a siege by French forces in 1756.

✚ 23K ☎ 971 36 21 00 🕐 Jun–Sep: guided tours ✋ Moderate

FORTALESA DE LA MOLA

The fortress at La Mola, guarding the entrance to Maó harbour, was built between 1850 and 1876 after the destruction of Fort Sant Felip (➤ above). During the Civil War and the Franco dictator-ship, it became a military and political prison where many exe-cutions took place. The army abandoned the fort in 1998 and it is now open for tours; allow at least two hours. You see the galleries, walls, casemates and gunpowder stores, as well as two 38cm (15in) Vickers cannons, the largest guns to be used in Spain – though they were never fired in defence as the fortress never came under attack.

www.fortalesalamola.com

✚ 24K ☎ 971 41 10 66 🕐 Jun–Sep Tue–Sun 10–8; May, Oct Sun 11am; Nov–Apr 10–2 ✋ Moderate

a walk from Es Castell

Start in Plaça de S'Esplanada, from outside the town hall.

Facing the military museum (▶ 96), head right along Carrer Cales Fonts. Turn right into Miranda de Cala Corb and follow the promenade, down to the harbour at Cala Corb and climb the steps to Carrer Sant Cristòfol on the far side. At the end of this road turn left. Cross the roundabout and walk uphill. Turn left at the crossroads; just after Carrer des Fusters on the left, the road bends right.

Turn left at the entrance to the *depuradora* (water treatment plant) on a country lane that continues across farmland between walls, eventually reaching a road.

Cross the road and take the track opposite; when this joins another road bear right. Passing a military base, turn left on to a wide track marked Horts de Binissaida. At the end of this track, go left on a walled path – when the wall on your right runs out, climb through a gap and follow the footpath towards the sea.

Soon you drop down to Cala de Sant Esteve (▶ 94), arriving beside the entrance to Fort Marlborough.

Walk around the bay and climb the narrow path at the far end to rejoin the road. Turn right at the cemetery. This road skirts the Sol del Este estate before reaching a small cove. Drop down to the beach then climb up the other side; continue

through a modern estate and over another road. Turn right at the T-junction to reach Cales Fonts for lunch; from here, Carrer Stuart leads back to the main square.

Distance 10km (6 miles)
Time 2.5 hours
Start/end point Es Castell ✚ 23K 🚌 Bus from Maó (Mahón)
Lunch Miramar (€€) ✉ Cales Fonts 38 ☎ 971 36 46 43

PUNTA PRIMA

The southeastern extremity of Menorca boasts one of the island's largest and finest beaches – but the currents in this part of Menorca can be dangerous and swimmers should pay particular attention to the Red Cross flag and only swim if the green flag is flying.

This is a popular area for water sports – you can rent wind- and kite-surfing and sailing equipment, as well as pedal boats on the beach. Facing Punta Prima across the sea is the Illa de l'Aire, an uninhabited island with an automatic lighthouse, clear sea-beds for diving and a small harbour for yachts. The island is the home of a rare species of black lizard.

➕ 23M ▮▮ Restaurants and bars on the seafront (€–€€) 🚌 Buses from Maó (Mahón) and Sant Lluís in summer

SANT CLIMENT (SAN CLEMENTE)

Unusually for the Mediterranean, this is a self-contained community where many locals grew up in the village and have lived there ever since – though most now work in Maó or at the airport, just a Balearic slingshot away. The village has several good restaurants, a couple of English pubs and bars, plus the inevitable main square with palm trees at its corners and an 18th-century church with a 20th-century facade.

➕ 21K ▮▮ Bars and restaurants near the main square (€–€€€) 🚌 Buses from Maó ❓ Festa de Sant Climent – third weekend in Aug

SANT LLUÍS (SAN LUIS)

Even by Menorcan standards, Sant Lluís is white – when the sun is shining, it almost sparkles. Founded by the French in 1761 during their brief occupation of Menorca to provide housing for their troops, it is laid out in a grid style around a series of attractive

squares. The town was named after Louis IX, to whom the huge, whitewashed, buttressed church is dedicated; the west front contains the coats of arms of the French royal family as well as the Comte de Lannion, Menorca's first French governor.

A blue and white windmill, **Molí de Dalt,** seen as you enter the town from Maó, is now a small folk museum with a collection of old farm implements – the main square opposite the windmill contains a good children's playground. Despite having become virtually a suburb of Maó, Sant Lluís remains a quiet, pretty town with a laid-back atmosphere and, perhaps surprisingly given its origins, a large British community. The hamlet of Torret to the south contains some of the finest traditional rural houses on the island.

✠ 22L 🍴 Restaurants and bars in main street (€€)

🚌 Buses from Maó ❓ Festa de Sant Lluís – last weekend in Aug

Molí de Dalt

✉ Calle de Sant Lluís 4

☎ 971 15 10 84 🕐 Apr–Nov Mon–Fri 10–2, 6–8, Sat 10–1, Sun 11–1; Dec–Mar Mon–Sat 10–2, Sun 11–1

✋ Inexpensive

TALATÍ DE DALT

Like many of Menorca's
prehistoric monuments, Talatí
de Dalt blends so well into its
surroundings that it is difficult
to tell which of the piles of
stones are ancient and which
modern. A wild olive tree grows inside the *taula* precinct; bushes
sprout out of a *talaiot* and standing stones are scattered around a
field. The central *taula* is one of the largest in Menorca; a separate
pillar leans against it, probably a result of an accident. The site dates
from 1400BC, but it was
inhabited until at least Roman
times.

➕ 21J ✉ Signposted off the
Maó–Ciutadella road, 4km (2.5 miles)
from Maó 🌐 Apr–Oct daily 10–8,
free access in winter ✋ Moderate
🍴 None

TORELLÓ

Two sites separated by around
300m (1,000ft) and a millennium
of history are found in the
shadow of a modern airport. The
talaiot here, one of the largest in
Menorca, is often the first that
visitors see – it is visible from
incoming planes.

  Of more interest is the 6th-
century basilica, Es Fornàs de
Torelló, discovered in 1956 by
a farmer ploughing up his
fields. The church, built under

Byzantine rule, is protected by a corrugated iron roof – but you can walk around the viewing platform and marvel at the motifs of intricate peacocks, lions and palm trees on the mosaic floor. Parts of the altar survive, as does the baptismal font; the design suggests an African influence, indicating early links with the North African church.

➕ 21K 📧 Off the Maó–Sant Climent road ⓧ Free access 🍴 None

TREPUCÓ

On the outskirts of Maó are a massive *taula* and *talaiot*, which have stood for

3,000 years while invaders have come and gone. The *taula* here, 4m (13ft) high, is the tallest in Menorca. The complex is surrounded by a star-shaped wall, built by the Duc de Crillon in 1782 when the French were laying siege to Fort Sant Felip (➤ 97) and used Trepucó as their base. In 1931 the site was excavated by Margaret Murray, who found small boys playing on top of the overgrown *taula*. Visitors should not climb on the ruins.

➕ 23K 📧 Signposted off the Maó–Sant Lluís road ⓧ Free access 🍴 None

HOTELS

MAÓ (MAHÓN)
Capri (€€)
Modern, three-star hotel with a rooftop pool close to Plaça de S'Esplanada.

✉ Carrer Sant Esteve 8 ☎ 971 36 14 00; www.rtmhotels.com

Mirador des Port (€€)
Three-star hotel with pool and sea views, close to the city centre.

✉ Carrer Dalt Vilanova 1 ☎ 971 36 00 16

Orsi (€)
Small, bright and cheerful *hostal* in the city centre.

✉ Carrer Infanta 19 ☎ 971 36 47 51 ◷ Feb–Nov

Port Mahón (€€€)
The best hotel in the capital, in an imposing colonial-style building overlooking the port. Fabulous gardens and a pool.

✉ Avinguda Fort de l'Eau 13 ☎ 971 36 26 00; www.sethotels.com

BINIBECA (BINIBÈQUER) VELL
Binivell Park (€€)
Houses and apartments in this 'Mediterranean fishing village'.

✉ Urbanización Binibeca (Binibèquer) Vell ☎ 971 15 06 08 ◷ Apr–Oct

CALA D'ALCAUFAR
Alcaufar Vell (€€€)
Rural estate with four large rooms in an old farmhouse, and other rooms in various outbuildings. Small pool. Dinner is served in converted stables.

✉ Carretera de Cala Alcaufar (7km/4 miles) ☎ 971 15 18 74; www.alcaufarvell.com ◷ Mar–Nov

Xuroy (€€)
Charmingly old-fashioned two-star *hostal* with its own landing stage right beside the beach at Cala d'Alcaufar.

✉ Cala d'Alcaufar ☎ 971 15 18 20; www.xuroymenorca.com ◷ May–Oct

CALA DE SANT ESTEVE
Sant Joan de Binissaida (€€)
Rooms on a working farm with great views. The French owner/chef cooks dinner using lamb, pork and vegetables from the farm.

✉ Camí de Binissaida 108 ☎ 971 35 55 98; www.binissaida.com ⏰ Apr–Jan

ES CASTELL
Agamenón (€€)
Large, traditional seaside hotel with great views over Maó harbour.

✉ Carrer Agamenón 16 ☎ 971 36 21 50; www.sethotels.com ⏰ Apr–Oct

Almirante (€€)
The former home of Admiral Collingwood is filled with paintings, maps and memorabilia of British rule. Good harbour views.

✉ Carretera Maó–Es Castell ☎ 971 36 27 00 ⏰ May–Oct

Barceló Hamilton (€€)
Large, old-fashioned hotel in a quiet, central location, with swimming pool, gym and harbour views.

✉ Passeig Santa Agueda 6 ☎ 971 36 20 50; www barcelo.com

Son Granot (€€€)
Magnificent rural hotel in a restored 18th-century British mansion. Eight rooms, some with balconies and sea views.

✉ Carretera Sant Felip ☎ 971 35 55 55; www.songranot.com ⏰ May–Oct

PUNTA PRIMA
Insotel Club Punta Prima (€€€)
Sprawling, rather bleak five-star holiday village on the beach with restaurants, pools and children's clubs.

✉ Carrer Migjera ☎ 971 15 92 00; www.insotel.com ⏰ Apr–Oct

SANT CLIMENT
Matchani Gran (€€€)
A large farmhouse offering luxury accommodation on a sheep farm.

✉ Carretera Sant Climent–Binidali ☎ 971 15 33 00; www.menorcountryhouse.com ⏰ Apr–Oct

SANT LLUÍS

Biniarroca (€€€)

A 16th-century farmhouse filled with art and antiques. Some of the 12 rooms share a private garden and pool. A child-free retreat.

✉ Camí Vell de Sant Lluís ☎ 971 15 00 59; www.biniarroca.com
🕐 Mar–Oct

Binisafullet Vell (€€)

Eight rooms on a working farm between Sant Lluís and the south coast, with a small pool in the gardens. Outdoor activities.

✉ Carretera Binissafuller 64 ☎ 971 15 66 73; www.binissafullet.com

Son Tretze (€€)

This 18th-century farmhouse at the entrance to Sant Lluís has eight rooms and a pool. No children.

✉ Carrer Binifadet 20 ☎ 971 15 09 43; www.hotelmenorca.com

RESTAURANTS

MAÓ (MAHÓN)

Amadeus (€)

Coffee, sandwiches, snacks and drinks – a great place for people-watching in a corner of the main square.

✉ Plaça de S'Esplanada 57 ☎ 971 35 07 92 🕐 Daily 8am–11pm

Café Mirador (€)

Wonderful harbour views – just the place for a scenic snack.

✉ Plaça Espanya 2 ☎ 971 35 21 07 🕐 Mon–Sat 10am–late

Casanova (€€)

Fresh pasta and wood-fired pizzas at a buzzing waterfront trattoria.

✉ Moll de Ponent 15 ☎ 971 35 41 69 🕐 Lunch and dinner, Tue–Sun

Casa Sexto (€€)

Fishy *tapas* and seafood specialities – the owner flies in fresh seafood from his native Galicia and cooks it while you wait.

✉ Carrer Vassallo 2 ☎ 971 36 84 07; www.casasexto.com 🕐 Lunch and dinner; closed Sun dinner and Mon

Es Fosquet (€€€)

Intimate harbourside fish restaurant in an old cave with white-washed walls and an outdoor terrace. Daily selection of fresh fish, which might include sea bream, bass or Menorcan prawns.

✉ Moll de Llevant 255 ☎ 971 35 00 58 🕐 Lunch and dinner Wed–Sun

Gregal (€€)

Locals consider this one of the best restaurants in Cala Figuera.

✉ Moll de Llevant 306 ☎ 971 36 66 06; www.restaurantegregal.com
🕐 Lunch and dinner

Jàgaro (€€€)

Fresh seafood and views from the harbourside terrace are the attractions at this top-notch Cala Figuera restaurant.

✉ Moll de Llevant 334 ☎ 971 36 23 90 🕐 Lunch and dinner daily; closed Sun in winter

Latitud 40° (€€)

If you don't feel like eating in the cosy restaurant upstairs, any of the dishes from the international menu can be enjoyed in the bar downstairs, although the liberal smoking policy will not suit everyone.

✉ Moll de Llevant 265 ☎ 971 36 99 00 🕐 Daily 11am–2am

La Minerva (€€€)

See page 59.

Marivent (€€€)

Possibly the best of the numerous harbourside restaurants in Cala Figuera; tables on the terrace look down over the port. Mainly fish and seafood but there are also exquisite grilled meat dishes.

✉ Moll de Llevant 314 ☎ 971 36 98 01 🕐 Lunch and dinner; closed Tue

Meson del Puerto (€€)

Classic Basque seafood in a lively area beside the ferry port.

✉ Moll de Ponent 66 ☎ 971 35 29 03 🕐 Closed Sun

Il Porto 225 (€€)

Quality Italian food and friendly service for customers of all ages. Try the carpaccio or monkfish with chilli pizzeria. Good vegetarian options and an excellent wine list.

✉ Anden de Levante, 225 ☎ 971 35 44 26; www.ilporto225.com ⊕ Lunch and dinner

Thai Country Style ($$)

Sublime, authentic Thai food – some of the best you will taste outside Thailand, with excellent service. Coconut beef curry and prawns with chilli are two of the choices available.

✉ Moll de Llevant 274 ☎ 971 35 39 34 ⊕ Lunch and dinner

Varadero (€€€)

Swish, expensive harbourside restaurant offering designer paellas and fish dishes such as monkfish casserole and oven-baked fish in a salt crust. Beside the jetty where cruise ships disembark.

✉ Moll de Llevant 4 ☎ 971 35 20 74 ⊕ Lunch and dinner

BINIBECA (BINIBÈQUER) VELL
Los Bucaneros (€€)

Old-style *chiringuito* (beach bar) with a bamboo-shaded terrace and a simple menu of salads, sandwiches, burgers and fresh fish.

✉ Platja de Binibèquer ⊕ May–Oct 10–8

El Pescadito (€€)

This 'little fish' restaurant serves a whole range of good, fresh fish and seafood, making it popular with locals and tourists alike.

✉ Poblado Pescadores 1 ☎ 971 15 09 70 ⊕ Lunch and dinner

CALA MESQUIDA
Es Cap Roig (€€)

Fresh fish, simply cooked, in a spectacular setting looking out to sea. The people of Maó come for a treat at weekends.

✉ Just before the village on the road from Maó ☎ 971 18 83 83
⊕ Tue–Sun 11am–midnight

ES CASTELL

Ca'n Delio (€–€€)

A good place to eat fresh grilled fish beside the sea. Excellent value; menu changes daily.

✉ Cales Fonts 38 ☎ 971 35 17 11 🕐 Lunch and dinner

El Italiano (€€)

Classic Italian cooking in a country house – risottos, pasta with truffles, Spanish and Italian wines. Children can ask for half portions.

✉ Carretera Sant Felip ☎ 971 36 53 10 🕐 Dinner only

España (€)

The locals come here for solid, unpretentious Menorcan and Spanish food.

✉ Carrer Victori 48 ☎ 971 36 32 99 🕐 Lunch and dinner

La Caprichosa (€–€€)

Harbourside pizzeria with pasta, meat and fish dishes and a special children's menu. Fish soup a speciality. Set menu tends to feature non-Italian dishes.

✉ Cales Fonts 44 ☎ 971 36 61 58 🕐 Lunch and dinner

Sa Foganya (€€)

Just above the fish restaurants by the harbour. Cured sausages, charcoal-grilled meat and vegetables are cooked on a hot slab at your terrace table. Good wine list.

✉ Carrer Ruiz y Pablo 97 ☎ 971 35 49 50 🕐 Thu–Tue 12–12

Sa Vinya (€–€€)

Wine, cheese and nibbles in a cave bar on the waterfront – just the place for an early-evening aperitif by the sea followed by a bargain set menu of *tapas* and dessert.

✉ Moll d'en Pons 7 ☎ 971 35 03 84 🕐 Jun–Sep daily 6pm–1am

Sirocco (€€)

See page 59.

Trébol (€€)

The best-known fish restaurant in Es Castell, and a night-time haunt of visiting celebrities. Sunny terrace or a shady cave.

✉ Cales Fonts 43 ☎ 971 36 70 97 🕐 May–Oct lunch and dinner

SANT CLIMENT
Es Molí de Foc (€€€)

Sophisticated Spanish cuisine in a town house with a pretty garden and modern art.

✉ Carrer de Sant Llorens 65 ☎ 971 15 32 22; www.molidefoc.com 🕐 Lunch and dinner

SANT LLUÍS
Biniarroca (€€€)

Elegant restaurant in a rural hotel offering fresh Mediterranean cuisine and produce from their organic gardens. Booking essential.

✉ Camí Vell de Sant Lluís ☎ 971 15 00 59; www.biniarroca.com 🕐 May–Oct dinner only; closed Tue

La Caraba (€€)

One of the top restaurants on the island offers modern Mediterranean cuisine in a country house. Fresh fish and unusual meat dishes like *carpaccio* of ostrich with Mahón cheese.

✉ S'Uestrà 78 ☎ 971 15 06 82 🕐 Jun–Sep Mon–Sat dinner

La Rueda (€€)

Right in the centre of town; a wide selection of *tapas* in the downstairs bar, a restaurant serving Spanish specialities upstairs.

✉ Carrer Sant Lluís 30 ☎ 971 15 03 49 🕐 Lunch and dinner; closed Tue

SHOPPING

ARTS AND CRAFTS
Francisco Lora

Francisco Lora's pottery, which is traditional Menorcan, but with distinctly modern touches, and a wide range of crafts and souvenirs.

✉ Moll de Ponent 33–36, Maó ☎ 971 35 03 03

La Maravilla
'The Marvelous' is aptly named and stuffed full of unusual and pretty gifts – most of them impractical.
✉ Portal de Mar 7, Maó ☎ 971 36 74 74; www.lamaravilla.es

S'Escopinya
Harbourside boutique specializing in Lladró porcelain.
✉ Cales Fonts 1, Es Castell ☎ 971 36 76 92

FOOD AND DRINK
Colmado La Palma
Delicatessen with a good selection of Mahón farmhouse cheeses as well as Menorcan sausages, biscuits, gin and Spanish wines.
✉ Costa de Sa Plaça 15, Maó ☎ 971 36 34 63

El Turronero
This shop has specialized in *turrón* (nougat) since 1894, and also sells Menorcan sausages, cheese and wine.
✉ Carrer Nou 22, Maó ☎ 971 36 28 98; www.elturronero.com

JEWELLERY
Joies de la Mar
Rita Pabst sells her own marine jewellery, with unusual designs incorporating seashells and coral.
✉ Moll de Llevant 176, Maó ☎ 649 23 88 13

Lopez
A wide selection of silver and jewellery, including Majórica pearls from Mallorca.
✉ Carrer Ses Moreres 58 and 60, Maó ☎ 971 36 04 78

Santa Capo
Artisan jeweller who skilfully fuses time-honoured techniques with striking, contemporary design. A good choice of silver and gold, often textured, pieces.
✉ Rector Mort 22b, Maó ☎ 971 36 63 40

LEATHER AND FASHION
Es Macar
One of the largest selections of Pou Nou cottonwear, with
T-shirts, shorts, summer dresses, hats and beach gear all in funky
local designs.

✉ Calle Hannover 50, Maó ☎ 971 36 55 52

Jaime Mascaró
Menorca is well regarded for its leather and this is the Maó branch
of the island's best-known shoe manufacturer; the shop also sells
leather jackets and bags.

✉ Dr Orfila 19, Maó ☎ 971 36 05 68; www.mascaro.com

Mark's
Handbags, belts, suitcases and jackets, sold at two shops in the
city centre.

✉ S'Arravaleta 18 and Costa de Sa Plaça 38, Maó ☎ 971 36 26 60;
971 36 56 25

Vives
Leather shoes and accessories.

✉ S'Arravaleta 16, Maó ☎ 971 36 28 46

SUPERMARKET
Eurospar
Convenient for the centre of town, this international chain
offers a decent selection of snacks and drinks and is open in
the evenings.

✉ Plaça Claustre del Carme 44, Maó ☎ 971 369 380

ENTERTAINMENT

BARS AND CLUBS
Akelarre
This waterfront bar attracts a sophisticated yachting crowd with
its laid-back music and occasional live jazz.

✉ Moll de Ponent 42, Maó ☎ 971 36 85 20 🕐 Daily 8pm–4am

Café Baixamar
Late-night meeting place that serves *tapas* throughout the day on the waterfront.
✉ Moll de Ponent 17, Maó ☎ 971 36 58 96 🕓 Daily 8am–4am

Casino
Menorca's oldest jazz venue, with a large expat following. Sessions are held throughout the summer and visitors are encouraged to join in.
✉ Carrer Sant Jaume 2, Sant Climent ☎ 971 15 34 18 🕓 Jazz nights May–Oct Tue 9:30pm–1am

Es Cau
Bring your own instruments to this music bar, inside a cave. The emphasis is on folk music, including traditional fishermen's songs.
✉ Cala Corb, Es Castell 🕓 Daily from 10pm

CASINO
Casino Marítim
Menorca's only casino is close to the Port Mahón hotel, with a terrace overlooking the harbour and a lift entrance from the waterfront promenade on Cala Figuera. Passports are required to enter the casino; smart dress is expected.
✉ Moll de Llevant 287, Maó ☎ 971 36 49 62; www.casinomaritimo.es
🕓 Daily 8pm–5am

DISCOS
Discoteca Si
A late-night place up the hill, playing everything from house to Spanish disco.
✉ Carrer de la Verge de Gràcia 16, Maó ☎ 971 36 00 04

Mambo
A cross between a funky bar and disco with thumping music and a large outside terrace.
✉ Moll de Llevant 209, Maó ☎ 971 35 18 52

THEATRE
Teatre Principal
An elegant opera house with films, plays and a spring opera season. For the best views book a seat in one of the 80 boxes.

✉ Costa d'en Deià 46, Maó ☎ 971 35 57 76

SPORT

BOAT TRIPS
Rutas Maritimas de la Cruz
One-hour trips around the historic port on a modern catamaran, and half-day trips exploring the coves and beaches of the east coast.

✉ Port de Maó, Maó ☎ 971 35 07 78; www.rutasmaritimasdelacruz.com

DIVING SCHOOLS
Diving Center
A modern dive centre with twice-daily dives suitable for all abilities.

✉ Passeig Marítim 44B, Fornells ☎ 971 37 64 31; www.divingfornells.com

S'Algar Diving
Specializes in cave diving. Also offers snorkelling trips for non-divers.

✉ Urbanización S'Algar, Cala d'Alcaufar ☎ 971 15 06 01; salgardiving.com

HORSE RACING
Hipódromo de Maó
Trotting races are held here throughout the year, on Saturday at 6pm in summer and Sunday at 10:30am in winter.

✉ Carretera Maó–Sant Lluís, Maó ☎ 971 36 57 30

KAYAKING
Menorkayaking
Guided kayak tours through secluded bays, as well as mountain-bike trips and walking tours.

✉ Carrer de sa Mitgera 8, Punta Prima ☎ 971 15 95 49;
www.menorkayaking.com

Eastern Central Menorca

This region has two main towns at its heart – Alaior and Es Mercadal. Alaior is Menorca's third town and is a pleasant place to visit. To the northwest is Es Mercadal, a qulet town that tourism has largely passed by.

On the south coast is Son Bou, the longest beach in Menorca, a complete contrast to the usual little coves dotted along the south. Other highlights along this part of the coast are the Bronze Age caves of Calcs Coves, used as dwellings and burial chambers; there are further prehistoric sites just inland. The north coast of this region is diverse. Here you will find the archetypal fishing village of Fornells, some of the wildest and windiest places on the island and the fascinating wetland area of S'Albufera d'es Grau.

Alaior

ALAIOR

Menorca's third largest town, 12km (7.5 miles) west of Maó, was founded by Jaume II of Mallorca in 1304 when he divided the island into seven regions, each with a central market town. The existence of Roman roads around the town, and the wealth of prehistoric remains nearby, suggest that it was a centre of population much earlier.

There are few specific sights in Alaior, but it makes a pleasant place to stroll – a town of gleaming white houses huddled together in narrow streets which lead up to the parish Church of Santa Eulàlia at the town's summit. Jaume II built the first church here; it was later fortified by villagers following the Turkish attacks on Maó (Mahón) and Ciutadella (Ciudadela). The present baroque church dates from the 17th century.

Another 17th-century church, Sant Diego, was once a Franciscan convent – its peaceful cloisters have been turned into modern flats, set around a courtyard with an old well at its centre. You can enter the cloisters via a vaulted, whitewashed alley beside the church. The style is said to be based on the Spanish colonial missions in Mexico and California. The courtyard, now known as Sa Lluna, is the setting for concerts and folk dancing in summer.

Alaior is an important centre for the manufacture of shoes, ice cream and especially Mahón cheese (► 14). You can buy cheese at the Coinga factory shop, which is signposted as you enter the town from the south. The shop sells the full range from *fresco* (fresh and soft) to *añejo* (matured for two years and as strong as Parmesan), as well as various cheesy souvenirs and jars of cheese in olive oil.

🚹 20H 🍴 Bars and cafés; Cobblers restaurant (€€) 🚌 Buses from Maó and Ciutadella ❓ Market Mon, Thu; Festa de Sant Llorenç Sun following 10 Aug

ARENAL D'EN CASTELL

This popular holiday centre is the most westerly of the trio of resorts reached by heading north from Alaior. Each of the three has its own distinct character and Arenal (the name means 'sandy place') is the brash one. The setting is superb – a near-circular bay with a long arc of fine sand backing on to dunes and pine-fringed cliffs – but it is rather spoiled by the presence of two enormous modern hotels towering over the beach. There is wind- and kite-surfing and water-skiing; you can rent pedal boats, motorboats, parasols and sunbeds. The shallow water and the presence of a first-aid post make this a relatively safe beach for children.

10C Bars and cafés; Cobblers restaurant (€€) Buses from Maó and Ciutadella Festa de Sant Llorenç Sun following 10 Aug

CALA EN PORTER

The setting is lovely – a wide beach leading to a narrow cove where almost unbelievably turquoise water shimmers between tall limestone cliffs. A *barranc*, or ravine, enters the sea via the marshland at the back of the beach. The western side is totally undeveloped, with cliffs tumbling into the sea; the eastern side must once have been the same but the cliffsides are now covered with villas and bars. The most unusual bar is Cova d'en Xoroi, a succession of stairways and rock platforms in a natural cave high in the cliff-face with dramatic views over the bay and out to sea.

➕ 19K 🍽 Bars and restaurants (€–€€) 🚌 Buses from Maó in summer

CALA PRESILI

A short walk from the headland at Cap de Favàritx (➤ 122–123) brings you to several quiet coves, beginning with Cala Presili. You start the walk by passing through wooden gates between a pair of white pillars 1km (0.5 miles) from the lighthouse. Cala Presili leads on to Cala Tortuga and then to Cala Morella Nou. All have high grassy dunes, white sand and good swimming – and none of them ever gets crowded. Behind the beach at Cala Tortuga is a marshy lake, part of the S'Albufera d'Es Grau nature reserve (➤ 50–51).

➕ 12D 🍽 None

CALA TIRANT

This pair of beaches between Fornells and Cap de Cavallería is reached either by taking the sign to 'Platges de Fornells' just outside Fornells and driving through the Menorca Country Club, or by following the dusty track 2km (1.2 miles) along the road to Cavallería which leads to the main beach. Both beaches are backed by dunes, marshland and a lake that attracts wading birds. The larger beach has a bar where you can rent umbrellas and sunbeds; there are also facilities for windsurfing and catamaran sailing. Swimming is safe and this is a good beach for children.

➕ 8B 🍽 Beach bar/restaurant in summer (€€)

CALES COVES

It takes an effort to get there – a rough four-wheel-drive track or a brisk 45-minute walk through the olive trees from Son Vitamina – but when you arrive at Cales Coves you are greeted by one of the most memorable sights on Menorca. The cliffs looking down on to this sheltered bay are home to more than 100 Bronze Age caves, carved out of the rock and used as both burial chambers and dwellings, with the living and the dead housed side by side. The oldest caves, seen on the left as you arrive, date back to the ninth century BC; follow the footpath over the rocks on your right to reach a second cove, passing more modern caves (4th century BC) whose features include windows, patios and interior cubicles. Some of these have Roman inscriptions, indicating that they continued to be occupied after the Talaiotic period. In recent years, a number of the caves have been illegally inhabited by squatters and latter-day troglodytes. After several unsuccessful attempts to evict these modern cavemen, the authorities barred access to the caves in 2001. Unfortunately this means that it is not usually possible to see inside.

The prehistoric villagers chose a good site – the angle of the coves means they are hidden from the open sea. This also provides safe mooring for pleasure boats in summer. The beaches are pebbly rather than sandy, but there is good swimming from the rocks.

➕ 20K 🍴 None 🚌 Buses from Maó and Cala en Porter to Son Vitamina in summer

CAP DE CAVALLERÍA

This headland at Menorca's northernmost point is one of the island's wild places. To get there you have to follow a potholed road across several kilometres of rocky moors, populated by wild goats. On the way you pass the tiny harbour of Sanitja. In Roman times this was the port of Sanisera, Menorca's third city. The results of recent excavations can be seen at **Ecomuseu Cap de Cavallería,** on the estate of Santa Teresa close to an old Roman settlement. Crossing cattle grids and passing through farm gates, eventually you reach the lighthouse at the end of the cape. Access to the lighthouse is barred but you can explore the headland on foot – if you can stand up in the wind. As you drive back towards civilization, the hills around Monte Toro loom up like a much larger range of mountains than they actually are.

🚩 8A 🍴 Café (€)

Ecomuseu Cap de Cavallería

☎ 971 35 99 99; www.ecomuseodecavalleria.com

🕐 Apr–Jun, Oct daily 10–7; Aug, Sep daily 10–8:30

💷 Inexpensive

CAP DE FAVÀRITX

Stand on Menorca's northeastern tip when the *tramuntana* is blowing and you will appreciate the island's savage beauty. Waves crash against crumbling slate cliffs, throwing sea-spray high into the air, and the solitary lighthouse acts as a reassuring reminder of humanity. The road from Maó is wide at first but eventually deteriorates into a bumpy track which in the end is little more than a causeway across the beach. From the cliffs at the end of the road you look out over an endless Mediterranean Sea. There are several pleasant quiet beaches which can be easily reached on foot from here, beginning with Cala Presili (➤ 119).

✚ 12D ❌ None

ES MERCADAL

The name of this town gives away its origins – it was founded in the 14th century as a central market halfway between the ports of Maó and Ciutadella. Much later it was the setting for a defining moment in Menorcan history, when a meeting of his supporters in 1706 declared the Austrian archduke Charles, pretender to the Spanish throne, to be king – providing the pretext for the subsequent British invasion and occupation.

Nowadays Es Mercadal is a quiet town of white houses in the shadow of Menorca's highest mountain, Monte Toro (➤ 42–43). The main industries are the manufacture of *abarcas*, local sandals with soles made from recycled tyres, and the almond biscuits *amargas* and *carquinyols*.

This is a sleepy place that has mostly been untouched by tourism. Carrer Major, the old main street, is a long pedestrian thoroughfare which climbs gently from the central square past white-walled, green-shuttered houses. At the top of Carrer Major is an old windmill (➤ 134), one of several restaurants in the town specializing in traditional Menorcan cuisine.

✚ 8D ❌ Jeni Restaurant (€) 🚌 Buses from Maó and Ciutadella ❓ Festa de Sant Martí third Sun in Jul. Craft market Thu evenings in summer

FORNELLS

Best places to see, ➤ 40–41.

MONTE TORO

Best places to see, ➤ 42–43.

NA MACARET

This old-fashioned seaside village 10km (6 miles) north of Alaior was one of the first Menorcan beach resorts in the 19th century – hence it avoided much of the vulgarity of the resorts that were developed much later. Rows of two-storey waterfront cottages face on to a small, sandy beach and a long narrow inlet which provides a perfect haven for yachts. There has been some recent development but it is relatively restrained.

🚩 11C 🍴 Two restaurants by the beach (€€)

PORT D'ADDAIA

Menorca's third-longest natural harbour, more than 3km (2 miles) long and 400m (1,300ft) wide, is popular with the yachting set

because of the protection it provides from the *tramuntana* wind. John Armstrong, who wrote the first English guide to Menorca in 1752, described this as the most perfect place on the island, and it is certainly very attractive. From the marina you look out across the masts of the yachts to a long, woody inlet and a sea framed by cliffs and small islands. This was the site of the final British invasion of Menorca in 1798, when Britain managed to capture the island without loss of life following the destruction of Fort Sant Felip by the Spanish. Inevitably a resort has mushroomed above the marina but the waterside itself remains blissfully unspoiled.

➕ 11D 🍴 Waterside restaurants and bars (€–€€)

RAFAL RUBÍ

Most people head for the Naveta des Tudons (➤ 44–45) to see the best-preserved example of a burial *naveta*; but it can be just as exciting to discover the lesser Bronze Age sites away from the beaten path. Signposted down a country lane on the main highway 7km (4.5 miles) west of Maó (Mahón), Rafal Rubí consists of two *navetas* set in the middle of farmland.

✚ 21J 🎟 Free access 🍴 None

S'ALBUFERA D'ES GRAU

Best places to see, ➤ 50–51.

SA TORRETA

One of the few Talaiotic sites in northern Menorca is also one of the hardest to reach; the best way is to walk from Es Grau (➤ 128), which takes you through rural farmland to the farm of the same name. Overgrown and evocative, a complete *taula* 4m (13ft) high is surrounded by standing stones on the edge of a farm. Tests show that this was built a thousand years after the *taulas* at Son Catlar (➤ 179) and Trepucó (➤ 103) – so the Talaiotic culture was certainly not short-lived.

✚ 12E 🎟 Free access 🍴 None

SHANGRI-LA

The name means 'an imaginary paradise', and imaginary it has turned out to be. Conceived in the tourist boom of the 1970s as an upmarket golf resort on the shores of the S'Albufera lake (➤ 50), Shangri-La was the subject of years of legal and political argument before being finally halted on the grounds that it represented illegal development in a conservation area. By this time many of the houses had been built; some were already lived in. The victory for Menorca's environmental campaigners proved to be a landmark, as the island realized that tourism had to be controlled. But a half-built *urbanización* is even worse than

a finished one, and if you wander around Shangri-La today you are bound to be struck by the air of desolation. Most visitors, however, are birdwatchers who are passing through this development on the edge of pine woods to spot birds in the S'Albufera d'Es Grau (➤ 50–51).

✚ 22H ⅰ None 🚌 Buses from Maó to Es Grau in summer

a walk to Sa Torreta

This walk has everything – countryside, archaeology, superb beaches and splendid coastal views.

Begin at Es Grau (➤ 50), walking around the beach to the far side opposite the car park. Climb the footpath on to the cliffs and turn right. The path rises and falls until you see Illa d'en Colom ahead. Follow the path down towards the sea, passing a cave house and crossing behind a small beach.

The path now swings left to cross a headland and drops to Fondeadero de los Llanes.

Walk around this bay, passing two inlets and a sandy beach, then up a slope on the far side. Climb over the wall to reach a sandy area and look for a narrow gap on the left leading to the cart-track. Note this spot carefully – there is a red arrow on a stone to guide you – and turn left.

An easy circular walk returns you to this spot. The track skirts the S'Albufera lagoon then climbs to Sa Torreta farm after 30–40 minutes.

At the farm, an overgrown path beside a concrete barn leads to Sa Torreta (▶ 126). Leaving the farm, take the track straight ahead. The track descends to Cala de Sa Torreta, shaded by pine woods, then climbs above the bay, passing another beach before turning inland. Now look for the junction where you began the circular walk. Turn left to return to Es Grau by the same route.

At Es Grau beach, go through the gap between the dunes to cross part of the S'Albufera reserve. You emerge on the main road a few minutes south of the village.

Distance 11km (7 miles)
Time 3 hours, plus picnic
Start/end point Es Grau ✚ 12E 🚌 Buses from Maó (Mahón) in summer
Lunch Take a picnic

SO NA CAÇANA (CASANA)

A short walk south of Torre Llisà Vell (► 132) on the Alaior to Cala en Porter road, this Bronze Age site with two *talaiots* and two *taulas* – both with their horizontal stone missing – is one of Menorca's least-visited archaeological sites. It is certainly not worth a detour, but if you have got out of your car already to see Torre Llisà Vell you may want to combine the two. Get there through a gap in the wall beside the main road.

✚ 20K ⊕ Free access ⑪ None

SON BOU

Best places to see, ► 52–53.

SON PARC

A dreary *urbanización*, with a golf course and hundreds of identical apartments, leads to this perfect beach, which is large enough not to get too crowded even in high summer. The water is shallow, there are pedaloes and motorboats for rent, and the dunes and pine woods at the back of the beach offer some relief from the sun. As so often in Menorca, there is also a peaceful cove just a short walk away from a busy resort. Take the path through a gap in the wall at the west end of the beach, walk for 20 minutes across the

headland breathing in the pungent mix of wild rosemary and salty sea breeze, cross a shingle beach, climb a hillock and then drop to Cala Pudent where, out of season, you can have the beach to yourself.

✚ 10C 🍴 Bar/restaurant in golf club (€€), and beach bar in summer 🚌 Buses from Maó (Mahón) and Fornells in summer

TORRALBA D'EN SALORT

This extensive site, 3km (2 miles) south of Alaior, is the closest Menorca has come to turning its prehistoric ruins into a tourist attraction. The road that used to bisect the site has been diverted, a car and coach park created, and arrows have been put up to guide visitors around Menorca's first archaeological park – the first ancient site in Menorca to levy an admission charge. There are the remains of a complete village here, including a *taula*, two *talaiots* and a Cyclopean wall, along with artificial burial caves. From the village there are good views of the white town of Alaior with Monte Toro (➤ 42–43) towering over it in the distance.

✚ 20J ✉ On the Alaior–Cala en Porter road 🕐 Jun–Sep daily 10–8; Oct–May Mon–Sat 10–1, 3–6 ✋ Moderate 🍴 Refreshment kiosk

TORRE LLISÀ VELL

This is the sort of place that makes seeking out Menorca's ancient monuments worthwhile – even if you have no interest in archaeology. Turn right off the Alaior to Cala en Porter road 5km (3 miles) south of Alaior at the crossroads marked 'Camí de Cutaines'; park at the farm and follow red arrows through the fields to reach the *taula* precinct, enclosed by its original wall. A perfectly preserved stone archway, perhaps 3,000 years old, guards the precinct – as you stoop beneath the ancient arch you wonder just how many people have stood there before you and why.

✚ 20J ⊕ Free access ¶¶ None

HOTELS

CALA EN PORTER
IBB Aquarium (€€)
Modern three-star hotel with pool and garden, right by the beach.
✉ Urbanización Cala en Porter ☎ 971 37 70 77; www.ibbhotels.com
🕐 May–Oct

ES MERCADAL
Jeni (€)
Simple but pleasant one-star *hostal* with a good Menorcan
restaurant and a rooftop pool; the only accommodation in town.
✉ Mirada del Toro 81 ☎ 971 37 50 59; www.hostaljeni.com

FORNELLS
Fornells (€€€)
Central three-star *hostal* with a pool. Most rooms have balconies
with sea views, and the restaurant serves fresh fish and lobster.
✉ Carrer Major 17 ☎ 971 37 66 76; www.hostalfornells.com

SON BOU
Sol Milanos Pinguinos (€€€)
A large modern hotel, catering mainly for families, with excellent
facilities, including a pool, restaurant and bar.
✉ Platja de Son Bou ☎ 971 37 12 00; www.solmelia.com

RESTAURANTS

ALAIOR
Cobblers (€€€)
Fresh, imaginative Mediterranean cuisine in the garden of a typical
Menorcan town house. Booking essential.
✉ Costa d'en Macari 6 ☎ 971 37 14 00 🕐 Apr–Oct dinner Mon–Sat

ES MERCADAL
Ca'n Aguedet (€€)
Considered one of the best restaurants on the island for traditional
Menorcan cuisine. Try the rabbit with figs.
✉ Carrer Lepanto 30 ☎ 971 37 53 91 🕐 Lunch and dinner

Ca'n Olga (€€)

Authentic Menorcan and Mediterranean cooking in a pretty town house with a summer terrace. Booking essential.
✉ Pont Na Macarrana ☎ 971 37 54 59 🕐 Dinner daily in summer, weekends only in winter

Molí des Reco (€€)

An old windmill at the top of the main street. In summer meals are served on the delightful terrace.
✉ Carrer Vicario Fuxà 53 ☎ 971 37 53 92 🕐 Lunch and dinner

S'Eixerit (€€)

Paella, grilled fish and a daily menu are served at this pretty garden restaurant in the centre of town.
✉ Carrer Tramuntana 29 ☎ 971 37 53 08 🕐 Lunch and dinner daily

ES GRAU
Es Moll (€€)

A superb setting on the waterfront, specializing in good seafood dishes, including grilled sardines.
✉ Moll Magatzems 17 ☎ 971 35 91 67 🕐 Lunch and dinner

FORNELLS
Ca'n Miquel (€€)

Small restaurant on the waterfront promenade; speciality rice and fish dishes, including the local spiny lobster.
✉ Passeig Marítim ☎ 971 37 66 23 🕐 Closed all day Mon and Sun dinner

Es Cranc (€€€)

Local seafood; hidden away in the town so more popular with locals than tourists.
✉ Carrer Escoles 31 ☎ 971 37 64 42 🕐 Lunch and dinner; closed Wed

Es Cranc Pelut (€€)

Serves the usual lobster, *paellas* and fish dishes but also has a good selection of meat dishes.
✉ Passeig Marítim ☎ 971 37 67 43 🕐 Lunch and dinner daily in summer

Es Pla (€€€)
See pages 58–59.

Es Port (€€€)
A good, reliable option, with a relaxed atmosphere. Like the other restaurants in Fornells, it specializes in fish and *caldereta de llagosta*.

✉ Gumersindo Riera 5 ☎ 971 37 64 03 🕐 Lunch and dinner

SHOPPING

ARTS AND CRAFTS
Galeria del Sol
Art gallery featuring work by foreign artists in Menorca.

✉ Via Ronda 28, Es Mercadal ☎ 971 15 40 07

FOOD AND DRINK
Ca'n Pons
Es Mercadal is known for its tasty almond macaroons, and this is one of the best establishments to buy them.

✉ Carrer Nou 13, Es Mercadal ☎ 971 37 52 58

Los Claveles
Pastry shop specializing in Menorcan and Arabic-style biscuits and sweets. Another branch by the main square in Ferreries.

✉ Carrer Nou 31, Es Mercadal ☎ 971 15 40 64; www.losclaveles.com

Queso Binibeca
Mature goat's cheese and Mahón cheese sold from the farmhouse. Signposted off the main road from Maó to Alaior.

✉ Carretera Maó–Alaior, km5.5 ☎ 971 36 92 44

Subaida
Quality cured meats, sausages, cheeses and jams have been produced by this company, which prides itself on its traditional methods, since 1843.

✉ Camí de Binifabini s/n, Es Mercadal ☎ 971 36 88 09; www.subaida.com
🕐 Mon–Sat 9–2

GIFTS
Balearica
Wide range of gifts, including shoes, bags and leather articles. There are also branches in Maó, Ciutadella and Fornells.

✉ Carretera Maó-Alaior, km 15, Alaior ☎ 971 37 27 36

Sa Farinera
Set in an old flour mill, the complex has an industrial museum as well as shops selling pottery, clothing and toys.

✉ Carretera Maó–Ciutadella, km 20, Es Mercadal ☎ 971 15 42 52; www.safarineramenorca.com 🕐 May–Oct daily 10–8

LEATHER
G Servera
Produces the local sandals known as *abarcas*, with leather uppers and a sole made out of recycled rubber tyres.

✉ Avinguda Metge Camps 3, Es Mercadal ☎ 971 37 53 84

ENTERTAINMENT

DISCO
Cova den Xoroi
A nightclub in a cave with terraces overlooking the sea.

✉ Cala en Porter ☎ 971 37 72 36; www.covadenxoroi.com 🕐 Fri, Sat 11pm–late

SPORT

DIVING SCHOOLS
Buceo Aventura
✉ Hotel Country Club, Fornells ☎ 626 47 67 78; www.divingmenorca.com

KAYAKING
Katayak
✉ Marina, Fornells ☎ 626 48 64 26; www.katayak.net

SAILING AND WINDSURFING
Windsurf Fornells
✉ Carrer Nou 33, Es Mercadal ☎ 971 18 81 50

Western Central Menorca

In the heart of this region is Ferreries, the highest town on the island, surrounded by farmland and with several outlets selling traditional produce. Close by is the dramatic gorge, Barranc d'Algendar, with its wildlife and challenging walks, while farther south is the attractive town of Es Migjorn Gran.

Ferreries

The coast to the south has some of the most unspoiled of Menorca's beaches, backed by pine and tamarisk woods. The north coast has some of the wildest scenery on the isalnd. Between the north and south coasts are more prehistoric sites to discover.

BARRANC D'ALGENDAR
Best places to see, ➤ 36–37.

BINIMEL-LÀ
Getting to Binimel-là is an adventure in itself. Head north from Es Mercadal along a series of country roads, then follow a wide dust track signposted to Binimel-là. After about 1.5km (1 mile) the track forks left to drop down to the beach, where you can park your car beside a freshwater lake. The beach, backed by sand dunes, is of red sand and pebbles; the water is deep and the absence of shade means you are exposed to the sun and wind. To escape this, head for the smaller sheltered beaches around the bay, popular with nudists – you can get there by ignoring the left fork mentioned above. The best reason for coming to Binimel-là, though, is in order to walk to Cala Pregonda (➤ 38–39).

✚ 7B 🍴 Bar/restaurant (€)

BINISUES (BINISSUÈS)
This stately home on the road to Santa Agueda, just west of Ferreries, has been turned into an exhibition of traditional

Menorcan life, customs and furniture. The home of the Salort y Martorell family, it retains its original furnishing and paintings, as well as farm buildings filled with old-fashioned tools. The top floor has interesting exhibitions of mounted butterflies, insects and birds, many of them endemic to Menorca. The name of the house, like so many in Menorca, reveals the island's Moorish past – *bini* is Arabic for 'sons of'. The restaurant here specializes in traditional Menorcan country cooking.

✠ 5D ✉ Off the C721 Maó–Ciutadella, km31 ☎ 971 37 37 28 ⏰ May–Oct Mon–Sat 11–6 🍴 Restaurant (€€) ✋ Moderate

CALA D'ALGAIARENS

These twin beaches on Menorca's remote northwest coast are reached by crossing the fertile La Vall region until you reach a pair of gateposts surmounted by offputting 'private' signs. In winter you are within your rights to drive on; in summer the landowner levies a toll, justified by the need to restrict traffic pollution in this environmentally sensitive area.

Once through the gates, follow signs to *'playa'* and when the track runs out, walk through the woods – a haven for migrant bee-eaters in spring and summer – to reach the sea. The main beach is a wide horseshoe of golden sand backed by dunes – you can scramble over the low rocks to reach a second beach, Platja d'es Tancats. Both beaches shelve gently into the sea and offer safe bathing in sheltered waters. This is a lovely, peaceful spot which only really gets busy at summer weekends. There are no facilities.

✠ 4B 🍴 None

CALA DEL PILAR

This is a wild, lonely, beautiful spot which nevertheless gets busy at weekends with locals trying to escape the crowds. Get there by leaving the main Maó (Mahón) to Ciutadella (Ciudadela) road from the 34km (21-mile) point beneath the Castillo Menorca factory shop; when the tarmac road runs out, you pass through some gates on to farmland and park in a thick grove of oak and pine. Walk for 40 minutes through the woods and you emerge on to reddish dunes; from here you can scramble down to the beach, or over the headland to the next cove. The woods reach almost to the beach and even the dunes are covered in vegetation. This is a conservation area and notices in several languages remind you to keep the beach clean.

✚ 5B ⊞ None

CALA EN TURQUETA

This beautiful spot could easily be destroyed by thoughtless development; as it is it remains blissfully unspoiled. The reason, as with so many of Menorca's beaches, is that it cannot be reached by road. Following a government campaign to reclaim Menorca's beaches, there is now a bumpy track leading to a free car park behind the beach, but this still feels like a place apart.

Pine-covered cliffs look down on to clear blue water and a beach of soft white sand backs on to extensive pine woods. The beach itself shelves gently into the sea, making it ideal for swimming. For the best views, climb on to the western cliffs – the path here continues to the next cove, Cala des Talaier, and from there to Arenal de Son Saura (➤ 173).

✚ 14H ⊞ None ⛴ Boat trips from Cala en Bosc and Ciutadella in summer

CALA ESCORXADA

Cala Escorxada is typical of the south coast – limestone cliffs, pine woods and a semicircular beach of soft white sand; it is also good for snorkelling. For many years the land behind Cala Escorxada was inaccessible because the landowner blocked access by erecting a series of barriers. Thanks to the island-wide Menorcan initiative to purchase land and open up the whole coast to visitors, this lovely little cove is now accessible to walkers willing to tramp the coastal footpath from Sant Adeodat (➤ 149).

✚ 16H ⁝⁝ None

CALA MACARELLA

A hike of around 30 minutes from the west end of Cala de Santa Galdana (➤ 144–145) across a fragrant headland covered with wild flowers and herbs ends in a wooden stairway leading down to this delightful cove where a *barranc* flows into the sea. It's a good way to escape the crowds in high summer but you won't be alone – there is a beach bar and there is even a rough road from Ciutadella that goes most of the way to the beach (it is a 20-minute walk from the car park). Pine trees reach almost to the water's edge, providing welcome shade, and the beach shelves gently into the sea, creating good conditions for swimming. Many people consider this one of the most perfect spots on the Menorcan coast.

Overlooking the bay on its western side are three large caves, once used as burial caves but now in service as holiday homes in summer. If you want more privacy, you can cross the headland above the caves to the even more perfect cove of Cala Macarelleta, where pine-fringed rocks surround a small sandy beach, popular with nudists. From the path on top of the headland you can look down on both coves at once, one of the best views anywhere on Menorca. The more adventurous can get between the two coves by swimming. Cala Macarella and Cala Macarelleta both offer good anchorage for yachts.

✚ 15H 🍴 Cafeteria Susy (€) 🚌 Buses from Ferreries, Maó (Mahón) and Ciutadella (Ciudadela) to Cala de Santa Galdana in summer

CALA MITJANA

Situated down a small rocky track, this popular beach can be reached by car or on foot from Cala de Santa Galdana (➤ 144–145). The walk starts in Plaça de Na Gran above the eastern end of the bay – climb up the steps from the beach and turn left. Take the gate leading out of the car park and stay on this clearly defined path which runs alongside a stone wall for much of the way. The walk takes about 30 minutes, passing the rocky cove of Cala Mitjaneta before arriving at a deep sandy beach surrounded by cliffs riddled with caves. The more adventurous can swim into some of the caves or leap from the cliffs into the cool blue water. The conditions here are also good for snorkelling.

✚ 15H 🍴 None 🚌 Buses from Ferreries, Maó and Ciutadella to Cala de Santa Galdana in summer

CALA PREGONDA

Best places to see, ➤ 38–39.

CALA DE SANTA GALDANA

One of Menorca's most beautiful (and ecologically important) coves is also one of the most developed – as such it has become a focus for debate about the extent of *urbanización* on the island. Thirty years ago there was not even a road here; now there are three enormous hotels and dozens of restaurants and bars.

The 'queen of the coves' takes its name from the Arab word for the local river; there is, in fact, no Saint Galdana. A wide arc of golden sand, bounded by wooded cliffs and an emerald sea, Cala de Santa Galdana enjoys a unique microclimate with higher temperatures and lower winds than the surrounding *calas*.

The Barranc d'Algendar (➤ 36–37) flows into the sea here, its mouth widened to form a marina for small boats. A footbridge across the stream leads to a rocky outcrop, almost an island, and a spectacularly sited bar-restaurant where you dine on a terrace directly overlooking the sea.

For the best views of the entire bay, follow the signs to Mirador de Sa Punta on the eastern cliffs, close to the start of the walk to Cala

Mitjana (► 143). You can also climb up here from the steps at the eastern end of the beach.

This is a good place to go in mid-season as a base for walks along the gorge or to some of the quieter beaches in both directions along the coast. In high season it is perfect for family holidays – fun and facilities for the children, safe swimming, and good shady walks for the adults. You can rent windsurfing and snorkelling equipment, pedaloes and motorboats, learn to sail or scuba-dive, or take a boat ride along the coast for a picnic at a peaceful cove.

🚼 15H 🍴 Wide choice of beachside restaurants (€€) 🚌 Buses from Ferreries, Maó (Mahón) and Ciutadella (Ciudadela) in summer

CALA TREBALÚGER

This classic south coast cove, fed by a freshwater stream from a limestone gorge, is one of the hardest to reach. A popular mooring for yachts and pleasure boats in summer, it can be reached only on foot by a walk of about 1.5 hours from Cala de Santa Galdana (➤ 144–145) followed by a scramble down to the beach.

✚ 16H 🍴 None 🚢 Boat trips from Cala en Bosc and Cala de Santa Galdana in summer

COVA DES COLOMS

An easy excursion can be made from Es Migjorn Gran (➤ below) to this remarkable cave in the Binigaus gorge. Follow the signs from the Sant Tomàs end of the town. From the car park, walk past the cemetery and along a wide track to the farm of Binigaus Vell, then look for a track on your left (marked *cuevas).* Clamber over the wall to your left at another *cuevas* sign and stay on this path for about 30 minutes' crossing the valley floor to reach the cave. It is dank, dark, the size of a cathedral and buzzing with birds and bats. The cave can also be reached on foot from the beach at Sant Adeodat (➤ 149).

✚ 17H 🍴 None 🚌 Buses from Maó (Mahón) and Cala en Porter to Son Vitamina in summer

ES MIGJORN GRAN

The name of this quiet village means 'the large town in the south', *es migjorn* being the local term for the low limestone plateau, broken by gorges, which dominates the landscape of southern Menorca. For 200 years the village was known as San Cristóbal, after a blacksmith who founded a township here in 1769 – but before that it was known locally as Es Migjorn Gran and it has reverted to its old name.

This is the only one of the inland towns not on the Maó–Ciutadella highway and it retains a certain provincial charm. The main street, Carrer Major, is like a painting of old Menorca – simple white houses with balconies and green shutters, the few houses in bright blues and yellows providing an attractive contrast. This is a sleepy spot, but the start of some good walks to the coast.

🚌 17H 🍴 Bars and restaurants (€–€€) 🚌 Buses from Maó and Ferreries, and a link to Sant Tomàs in summer ❓ Market Wed; Festa de Sant Cristòfol late Jul/early Aug

FERRERIES

The highest town in Menorca – 150m (490ft) above sea-level – was built in the shadow of the island's second-highest mountain, S'Enclusa (276m/905ft). The name of the mountain means 'anvil' and it is thought the town's name derives from the word for 'blacksmith' – this was probably a centre of smithing along the road from Maó (Mahón) to Ciutadella (Ciudadela). The main industries today are furniture and shoe manufacture; there are factory shops on the main road selling leather shoes.

Plaça d'Espanya, at the heart of the town, is a large modern square with a fountain and a children's play area. This is the venue for the popular farmers' market on Saturday mornings, with produce and craft stalls and folk-dancing displays in summer. East and south of here are the wide avenues of the new town, which has expanded greatly since the 1940s; west and north are the narrow streets of a typical Menorcan town, all white houses with green shutters and a 19th-century parish church. Less pretty than

its neighbours Es Mercadal and Es Migjorn Gran, Ferreries
has successful local industries meaning it is well-populated
throughout the year. It is also developing a reputation as a centre
for rural tourism; the **Museu de la Natura** has exhibitions on
environmental themes.

Just outside Ferreries is Son Mercer de Baix, an early Talaiotic
village overlooking the confluence of two gorges (➤ 150–151).

✚ 6D ⏹ Restaurants and bars in the town centre (€–€€) 🚌 Buses from
Maó and Ciutadella ❓ Market Tue and Fri; farmers' and craft market Sat;
Festa de Sant Bartomeu 23–25 Aug

Museu de la Natura
✉ Carrer Mallorca 2 ☎ 971 37 45 05 🕐 Tue–Sat 10:30–1:30, 5:30–8:30,
Sun 10–1 ✋ Inexpensive

SANT ADEODAT

The western end of
Sant Tomàs beach
(➤ 152–153), beyond
the road from Es Migjorn
Gran (➤ 146–147), is
totally undeveloped and
known as Sant Adeodat.
The sand is fine, the
swimming is safe but beach facilities are found at the more
popular Sant Tomàs. A short walk on a sandy path behind the
beach, passing the islet of Binicodrell offshore, brings you to the
larger beach at Binigaus, popular with nudists but with dangerous
currents that make it unsafe for swimming. From Binigaus you can
walk inland along the Barranc de Binigaus, a limestone gorge
riddled with caves, including the cathedral-like Cova des Coloms –
though the easier approach to this particular cave is from Es
Migjorn Gran.

✚ 17J ⏹ Beach bar in summer; restaurants at Sant Tomàs (€€) 🚌 Buses
to Sant Tomàs from Maó, Ciutadella and Es Migjorn Gran in summer

a walk near Ferreries

This walk takes you deep into a valley for a close-up look at one of Menorca's limestone gorges. It is strenuous but spectacular, and easy to follow.

Start at the farm of Son Mercer de Dalt, 2km (1.2 miles) from Ferreries (▶ 148–149) and reached by a wide track that begins 0.5km (0.3 miles) beyond the bridge on the road to Es Migjorn Gran. Take the track between the farmhouse drive and some barns, signposted Poblat de Son Mercer de Baix. After a few minutes, turn left on to a wide track; this passes through three gates then descends to the valley floor where you enter a lush field.

After 5 minutes you reach a secluded house. Cross the yard of the house, remembering to shut the gate, and continue on a lane above an orchard. When the lane divides, fork right to climb out of the valley. Climb for 20–30 minutes, then cross a cattle grid; a right turn at the next gate leads into a field and soon you see the farm of Son Mercer de Baix ahead. When you reach a junction with the farm on your right, turn left.

The next section is an optional extra but well worth it. An easy walk of around 1km (0.5 miles) brings you out at the prehistoric village of Son Mercer (open Sat), where you can picnic among the *talaiots* and look down over the valley to see how far you have climbed.

Return along the same track but continue straight ahead through the farmyard. In the distance you see the impressive farmhouse of Son Mercer de Dalt – your start point.

Distance 8km (5 miles)
Time 2.5 hours
Start/end point Son Mercer de Dalt 🚌 6E 🚌 Bus to Ferreries then walk for 2km (1.2 miles)
Lunch Take a picnic

SANT AGUSTÍ VELL

This is one of the hardest of Menorca's prehistoric sites to find but that makes the effort all the more rewarding and you will probably be alone with your thoughts when you get there. Take the road from Es Migjorn Gran to Sant Tomàs; after 1km (0.5 miles), an unsigned track to your right leads to the farm of Sant Agustí. Park just off the main road and walk along this track. At the farm gates, go right, through a gate marked *cuevas*; when you see a pair of litter bins you know that you have reached the site. The main attraction here is a large *talaiot* with a beamed roof of olive and juniper wood; once they would all have been like this but this is the only one that survives. The village was strategically situated at the head of the Binigaus gorge; it can also be reached by climbing from the Cova des Coloms (► 146).

✚ 17H ⊛ Free access 🍴 None 🚌 Buses to Es Migjorn Gran from Maó (Mahón) and Ferreries

SANT TOMÀS

This long beach of pale golden sand is virtually a continuation of the beach at Sant Adeodat (► 149). It is separated from the beach at Son Bou by a pair of low headlands. Once a quiet spot, it has grown into a major resort with four large hotels and an *urbanización* creeping up the hills behind the beach. In 1989 a freak storm blew away all the sand from the beach and what you see

now has been imported in its place. A path at the western end of the beach leads to the quieter beaches of Sant Adeodat and Binigaus (➤ 149). Take note of the flag system for safe bathing as the beach has dangerous currents.

✛ 17J 🍴 Beachside restaurants and bars (€€)
🚌 Buses from Maó, Ciutadella (Ciudadela) and Es Migjorn Gran in summer

SANTA AGUEDA

Climbing Menorca's third-highest hill today, there is little to suggest that it once supported the island's most significant fortress. Built by the Romans and strengthened by the Moors, the castle on Santa Agueda's summit was the last Muslim stronghold to resist the Catalan conquest in 1287. The buildings have fallen into disrepair and only the serious archaeologist would recognize the Roman, Arabic and Spanish influences – but it is still worth the walk up here for the views, which stretch to both Maó and Ciutadella and along the windswept north coast. As a bonus, the path to the summit takes you along the best preserved Roman road in Menorca. To get there, take the Binisues road, signposted off the C721 3km (2 miles) west of Ferreries; after another 3km (2 miles), park by an old white schoolhouse and go through the gate to begin your walk. The climb to the summit takes a brisk 45 minutes. This is a popular picnic spot, much used by local people at weekends.

✛ 6C 🍴 None

TORRE LLAFUDA

This little-visited site off the highway from Maó (Mahón) to
Ciutadella (Ciudadela) contains a complete *taula*, less than 2m
(6.5ft) tall and romantically surrounded by a halo of wild olive and
holm oak. Near the *taula* you will find burial caves and some well-
preserved defensive walls. Among the finds here was a Roman
gold ring engraved with the figure of a camel; like many prehistoric
sites, Torre Llafuda continued to be occupied well into Roman
times and possibly much later.

✚ 4D ✉ Signposted off the Maó–Ciutadella road at km 37 ⊘ Free access
🍴 None

TORRE TRENCADA

Drive across farmland on the old Roman road from Ciutadella to
Maó, turn into a small car park, cross three cattle grids and across
a field you catch sight of a monumental *taula* hiding among the
trees. Birds sing and cattle graze as you cross the field; the
prehistoric village is surrounded by drystone walls and as with so
many of Menorca's ancient sites it is hard to tell where the old
stones end and the new ones begin.

✚ 4D ⊘ Free access 🍴 None

HOTELS

CALA MACARELLA
Morvedra Nou (€€€)

Smart rural hotel close to the south coast beaches with 18 rooms; some in garden villas and others in the 17th-century house. Views stretch to Mallorca on a clear day. Bar, restaurant and pool.

✉ Camí de Sant Joan de Missa, km 7 ☎ 971 35 95 21; www.morvedranou.es 🕔 May–Oct

CALA DE SANTA GALDANA
Audax (€€)

Luxury four-star beach hotel with a rooftop pool and sea-facing balconies. The hotel's sports centre can arrange everything from bike rental to scuba-diving trips.

✉ Cala de Santa Galdana ☎ 971 15 46 46; www.rtmhotels.com 🕔 Mar–Oct

ES MIGJORN GRAN
58 S'Engolidor (€)

Four rooms in a family-run inn with a terrace overlooking a gorge. The restaurant serves excellent Menorcan cuisine.

✉ Carrer Major 3 ☎ 971 37 01 93; www.sengolidor.com 🕔 Apr–Oct

La Palmera (€)

Simple accommodation with shared bathrooms in a 19th-century house, now a theatre and bar.

✉ Carrer Major 83 ☎ 971 37 00 23

FERRERIES
Jeni (€€)

Apartment-hotel with its own pool in the centre of town.

✉ Mirada del Toro ☎ 971 37 41 81; www.hotel-jeni.de

Son Triay Nou (€€)

This pink, colonial-style farmhouse is now a rural hotel with four suites, plus a tennis court and swimming pool. The breakfast buffet features local produce.

✉ Carretera Cala Galdana ☎ 600 07 44 41; www.sontriay.com 🕔 Apr–Oct

SANT TOMÀS
Santo Tomàs (€€€)
Smart, four-star hotel close to the beach, with 85 rooms, a spa and a large swimming pool.

✉ Urbanización Santo Tomàs ☎ 971 37 00 25; www.sethotels.org
🕐 Apr–Oct

RESTAURANTS

CALA MACARELLA
Susy (€)
See page 59.

CALA DE SANTA GALDANA
Es Barranc (€€)
Traditional island cuisine, with the emphasis on fresh fish and seafood, is the speciality of this long-standing local restaurant.

✉ Cala de Santa Galdana ☎ 971 15 46 43; www.esbarranc.com 🕐 Lunch and dinner

El Mirador (€€–€€€)
See page 58.

ES MIGJORN GRAN
Ca Na Pilar (€€)
Imaginative Mediterranean cooking with a pretty garden terrace.

✉ Carretera Es Mercadal–Es Migjorn ☎ 971 37 02 12 🕐 Lunch and dinner; closed Wed

58 S'Engolidor (€€)
Fresh Menorcan cooking in an 18th-century town house, now a hotel (➤ 155), with a terrace overlooking a gorge. Book ahead.

✉ Carrer Major 3 ☎ 971 37 01 93 🕐 Dinner only; closed Mon

FERRERIES
Binisues (€€€)
Traditional Menorcan cookery including fresh fish dishes, served in an old manor house (➤ 138–139). Specialities include *caldereta*

de langosta (lobster stew), crayfish with beans and a fish and rice soup.

✉ Carretera Maó–Ciutadella, km 31 ☎ 971 37 37 31 ◷ Lunch and dinner daily in summer; weekends only in winter

Méson El Gallo (€€)

Charcoal grills are a speciality in this 200-year-old picturesque farmhouse. The steak with Mahón cheese is known throughout the island.

✉ Carretera Cala Santa Galdana, km 1.5 ☎ 971 37 30 39 ◷ Lunch and dinner; closed Mon

Mesón Rias Baixas (€€)

Fish features prominently on the menu at this small restaurant, but there's plenty of meat and traditional dishes too.

✉ Plaza Minorca 2 ☎ 971 37 45 58 ◷ Lunch and dinner

SHOPPING

ARTS AND CRAFTS
Galeria Migjorn Gran

Watercolours by British artist Graham Byfield, who lives in the village, and by other local artists.

✉ Carrer Sant Llorenc 12, Es Migjorn Gran ☎ 971 37 03 64

FOOD AND DRINK
Hort de Sant Patrici

This dairy farm just outside Ferreries offers tastings of unpasteurized farmhouse cheese as well as a cheese museum and the chance to see Mahón cheese being made.

✉ Camino Ruma, 1km (0.5 miles) north of Ferreries ☎ 971 37 37 02; www.santpatrici.com

LEATHER AND FASHION
Calzados Ferrerias

Ferreries is the centre of shoe and handbag production in Menorca and this shop sells the products of a local factory.

✉ Araders 2, Ferreries ☎ 971 37 30 21

Ca'n Doblas

Handmade shoes and *abarcas* (sandals) at a traditional workshop beside the town hall and parish church.

✉ Plaça Jaume II, Ferreries ☎ 971 15 50 21; www.candoblas.com

Jaime Mascaro

Large factory shop beside the Maó–Ciutadella highway, representing the best-known name in Menorcan shoes.

✉ Poligono Industrial, Ferreries ☎ 971 37 45 00; www.jaimemascaro.com

SPORT

DIVING SCHOOLS
Sea Gypsy Divers

Small, friendly operation offering two dives a day May–Oct, exploring more than 20 sites around Cala Galdana and beyond.

✉ Hotel Sol Galvilanes, Cala Galdana ☎ 629 73 48 73; www.seagypsydivers.com

HORSEBACK RIDING
Menorca a Cavall

Guided horse rides through peaceful countryside, as well as traditional horse carriage rides from a rural *finca.*

✉ Lloc de Santa Rita–Carretera Es Mercadal-Ferreries ☎ 971 37 46 37

MULTI-ACTIVITY
Audax Sports and Nature

The beach hut beneath the Audax hotel (➤ 155) offers sporting activities from canoeing and fishing to tennis, golf, scuba-diving and beach volleyball, along with boat trips, bicycle rides and guided walks.

✉ Passeig del Riu, Cala de Santa Galdana ☎ 971 15 45 48 ◷ Apr–Oct

SAILING
Blue Mediterraneum

Boat chartering and rental for a day or overnight.

✉ Cala de Santa Galdana ☎ 971 36 44 82; www.chartermenorca.com

Ciutadella and the West

Where Maó (Mahón) is bureaucratic, Ciutadella (Ciudadela) is artistic; where Maó has power, Ciutadella has style. The nobility and the church stayed behind when the capital was moved to Maó with the result that Ciutadella remains a pure Catalan city, undiluted by British or French architecture or the ideas that colonial rulers brought in their wake.

Ciutadella de Menorca

There were Carthaginian and Roman settlements here, and the Arabs made it their

capital, but Ciutadella, Menorca's second town, reached its zenith in the 17th century when the island's richest families settled here.

The coastal area to the west and south of Ciutadella comprises some of the busiest tourist complexes on the island. This is the closest Menorca gets to mass urbanization, but you can still seek out some pretty, quieter beaches away from the throngs. For history buffs, there are fascinating prehistoric caves on the north coast and inland a Bronze Age burial chamber and a megalithic settlement.

CIUTADELLA (CIUDADELA)

Wander Ciutadella's maze of narrow streets fanning out from the cathedral, their Gothic palaces each marked by a coat of arms carved above the door; sit beneath the palm trees in the Plaça des Born at dusk; join the citizens for their annual festival, when richly caparisoned horses prance through the streets, and you begin to appreciate the truth of the Count of Cifuentes' *bon mot* – 'Maó (Mahón) may have more people, but Ciutadella has more souls.'

✚ 2D

Castell Sant Nicolau

This 17th-century octagonal defence tower, with drawbridge, moat and turrets, stands alone on a limestone platform halfway around the Passeig Marítim (► 169). Nowadays it is used as an exhibition centre, with displays on environmental themes and occasional art exhibitions. The reason for coming here, though, is to watch the sun set over the sea and see the mountains of Mallorca appear, silhouetted against a pink sky.

✉ Passeig Marítim 🕐 Tue–Sat 10–1:30, 5–8 ✋ Free 🍴 None

Catedral

Ciutadella has been Menorca's religious capital since Arab times; when Alfonso III conquered the island in 1287, one of his first acts was to have the main mosque reconsecrated as a church. The Catalan-Gothic structure took shape over the next 75 years, though part of the old mosque still remains in the ramp of the north tower, reminiscent of an Islamic minaret. The church finally gained its cathedral status

in 1795, when a bishopric was restored to Ciutadella after an absence of 1,300 years.

Outside, a stark, windowless wall – probably added after the Turkish raid on Ciutadella in 1558 – leads to thick square buttresses. Inside, an aisleless nave leads to a pentagonal apse and a dozen side chapels. Most of the interior fittings were destroyed during the Spanish Civil War and what you see is heavily restored.

✉ Plaça de la Catedral ☎ 971 38 07 39 🖐 Free 🍽 In the square (€–€€)

Molí des Comte

First built in 1778 for the Count of Torre-Saura, Ciutadella's only surviving windmill fell into disrepair until it was restored in the 1960s. A winding 73 steps lead to the tower, where you can get a close-up look at the machinery and a view of the city's rooftops through the sails, though there is little to detain all but the most dedicated windmill enthusiast. The square opposite, Plaça Alfons III, is commonly known as Plaça de Ses Palmeres because of the palm trees which grow there.

✉ Camí de Maó 1 🕐 Jun–Sep Mon–Sat 10–1 🖐 Free 🍽 Bar Es Molí in the windmill (€–€€)

Museu Diocesà

The Museum of the Diocese of Menorca is housed in a former Augustine monastery close to the cathedral. Peaceful baroque cloisters lead on to a series of rooms containing ecclesiastical treasures including vestments, chalices and reliquaries. There is also a room with prehistoric finds, and a collection of paintings by the Catalan artist Pere Daura, born in Ciutadella in 1896.

Behind the museum, in Plaça de la Libertat, is the city's lively food market, with stalls selling fresh fruit, vegetables, meat, cheese and fish.

✉ Carrer Seminari 7 ☎ 971 48 12 97 🕐 Tue–Sat 10:30–1:30 🖐 Inexpensive 🍽 Nearby in Plaça de la Catedral (€–€€)

Museu Municipal de Ciutadella

The Bastió de Sa Font was built as a fortress in the late 17th century; it was subsequently used as a grain store, a gas factory and a water tank before being fully renovated and opened as the city's museum in 1995. The displays, neatly laid out in a long, bright, vaulted gallery, are carefully captioned and there are leaflets available in English to help you to find your way around.

The museum tells the history of Menorca from pre-Talaiotic to Muslim times through a collection of fascinating exhibits gathered from archaeological excavations around the island – bone knives which go back 3,000 years, ancient spears and slingshots, Roman coins, jewellery, oil lamps and dice. The most gruesome display case contains a collection of Iron Age skulls, which show that the Talaiotic culture had developed advanced techniques in cranial pathology. As well as head wounds caused by blows from weapons, there are fractures which are the result of trepanning, or surgery.

✉ Bastió de Sa Font ☎ 971 38 02 97; www.ciutadella.org/museum 🕐 Tue–Sat 10–2 (and 6–9 in summer) ✋ Inexpensive 🍴 In city centre (€–€€)

Museu del Pintor Torrent

José Torrent, a native of Ciutadella who was born in 1904, is widely considered one of the two greatest Menorcan painters of the 20th century – the other is Joan Vives Llull, from Maó. After his death in 1990, a number of Torrent's works were gathered together in an old town house close to the Plaça des Born. You can follow his development from youthful Impressionism to the Expressionism of his final years, and see for yourself why he is known as 'the Van Gogh of Menorca'.

✉ Carrer Sant Rafel 11 ☎ 971 38 04 82 🕐 Mon–Fri 11–1, 7:30–9:30, Sat–Sun 8pm–9:30pm ✋ Free 🍴 Nearby in Plaça des Born (€–€€)

a walk around Ciutadella

Begin in Plaça des Born (➤ 46–47), with your back to the town hall.

Go up Carrer Major del Born, directly facing the obelisk. Turn left in front of the cathedral along Carrer Ca'l Bisbe.

This takes you past the bishop's palace to Palau Squella, a fine 18th-century mansion.

Turn left at the end of the street, then right into Carrer Sant Rafel, passing the Museu del Pintor Torrent (➤ 165) and continuing into Carrer Sant Miquel. At the first crossroads, a narrow passage on the left leads to the old sea walls.

Look down on to Pla de Sant Joan, a large open space that is the venue for the city's main festival in June.

Turn right to reach the old fort, now the Museu Municipal (➤ 164–165), then turn right on to Carrer Portal de Sa Font. Passing the convent of Santa Clara (➤ 172), continue along the narrow street ahead then turn left into Carrer Sant Antoni to reach Plaça Nova.

Walk up to Carrer de Maó to Plaça Alfons III, a popular meeting place and a good lunch stop.

Turn right along the ring road at the end of the square, then right again into Carrer Alaior. At the market square turn right, then left into Carrer del Socors and left again into Carrer Seminari. At the end of this street turn right then right again into Carrer del Roser. When you reach the cathedral, turn left to return to Plaça des Born.

This walk can be combined with a pleasant stroll along the Passeig Marítim (▶ 169). Leave Plaça des Born on its southwest side to reach Plaça de S'Esplanada, a shady square of pine trees also known as Plaça dels Pins. From here you can drop down to the seafront promenade and follow it to its end. Return to Plaça de S'Esplanada along Carrer de Mallorca. Allow an extra hour.

Distance 2km (1.2 miles)
Time 1 hour
Start/end point Plaça des Born
Lunch Aurora (€€) ✉ Plaça Alfons III 3 (▶ 181)

Palaus

The streets of the old city are filled
with 17th-century palaces, built by
Menorca's aristocratic families
when they moved to Ciutadella
from their country estates. Most
are still owned by the original
families, in some cases the
descendants of those who were
rewarded in 1287 when Alfonso 'the
Liberal' divided up his new
conquest among his followers and
friends.

Peep into any of these palaces when the doors are open and you see fine courtyards with stone stairways, Italianate loggias and galleried arcades. Most are closed to the public, including the Torre-Saura palace on Plaça des Born, the Martorell palace on Carrer de Santíssim and the Palau Salord on Plaça des Born, but they are worth walking past for a glimpse.

🍴 In Plaça des Born (€–€€)

Passeig Marítim

This wide promenade, completed in 1997, follows the seafront around the peninsula from the small beach at Cala des Degollador to the marina. This is the place to come at dusk to watch the sun set over the sea and join the locals on their evening *passeig*. Mothers and grandmothers, teenagers holding hands – the whole population of Ciutadella seems to be there. As the promenade approaches the city centre, a flight of steps leads down to the port where you can walk around the harbour and look up above the old city walls to the Plaça des Born. Allow half an hour for the full promenade along the rocky, often windswept coastline. There are good views out to sea, apart from some people-watching during this sociable daily event. Do what the locals do and end up with a warming coffee or Spanish brandy at one of the cafés on Placa d'es Born before heading off for a seafood supper.

🍴 In the harbour (€€–€€€)

Plaça des Born

Best places to see, ➤ 46–47.

a drive from Ciutadella to Maó

The map of Menorca is dominated by one road, the Me-1, connecting Maó to Ciutadella. A drive along this road passes three inland towns and several prehistoric sites.

Start on the edge of Ciutadella, at the roundabout with the sculpture of a prancing horse.

Pass the football stadium and the industrial estate on your left, with factory shops competing for your attention. After 4km (2.5 miles) the car park for Naveta des Tudons (► 44–45) is reached on the right; shortly after this there are more turn-offs to Torre Trencada (► 154) and Torre Llafuda (► 154). After 9km (5.5 miles), skirt a crest by the shops of Castillo Menorca where you will have your first view of the central mountains.

After passing the manor house of Binisues (➤ 138), a series of bends takes you up to Ferreries (➤ 148–149). The road continues to Es Mercadal (➤ 123), with Monte Toro (➤ 42–43) dominating the view.

After bypassing Es Mercadal, Camí d'en Kane leads off to the left; next you climb a twisting hill to a picnic area overlooking the rock formation known as Sa Penya de S'Indio, because of its apparent resemblance to an Indian brave. From here the road bypasses Alaior (➤ 116), then goes fast and straight to Maó.

Keep straight ahead at the industrial estate, following signs for 'Centre Ciutat'. Bear right at the mini-roundabout to reach Plaça de S'Esplanada, the start of the walk around Maó (➤ 88–89).

You can return to Ciutadella the same way; combine this with one of the other drives or take the country roads between Es Mercadal and Ferreries via Es Migjorn Gran (➤ 146–147).

Distance 44km (27 miles) one way
Time 1 hour
Start point Ciutadella ✚ 2D
End point Maó ✚ 23K
Lunch Molí des Racó (€€) ✉ Carrer Vicario Fuxà 53, Es Mercadal

Santa Clara

Founded by Alfonso III immediately after the Reconquest in 1287, this convent was destroyed during the Turkish attack on Ciutadella in 1558 and rebuilt 56 years later. It was destroyed again during the Spanish Civil War and the building you see today dates from 1945.

It is still a working convent and only the church is open to visitors; it is plainly decorated with white stone

arches and the kaleidoscopic altarpiece, with its dazzling rainbows and purple skies, comes as quite a shock.

✉ Carrer Portal de Sa Font ☎ 971 38 27 78 ⏰ Daily 6–1:30, 4:30–8:30 🍴 Nearby (€–€€) ✋ Free

Ses Voltes

This pedestrian alley at the heart of the old city, also named after the local historian José-Maria Quadrado, is the focal point of Ciutadella's social life. This is where café life reigns, as people spend their siesta sitting on canvas chairs in the shade of Moorish-style arches, then return during the evening passeig for a drink outside one of the bars on Plaça Nova before checking out the row of billboards to see what is on at the cinema.

🍴 Lots of restaurants and bars in Plaça Nova (€–€€)

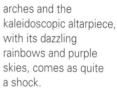

More to see in the West

ARENAL (PLATGES) DE SON SAURA

One of Menorca's prettiest beaches is also one of the hardest to reach. To get there by car you have to cross farmland and in summer the farmer levies a toll; this is one of the last remaining beaches where the island government has not yet managed to buy up the land in order to create free access. If you don't want to drive, you can walk from Cala en Turqueta (1 hour) on the coastal footpath from Son Xoriguer to Cala de Santa Galdana. It is worth the effort – two long stretches of white sand, hidden behind fragrant pine woods and neatly divided by a woody outcrop. There are no beach facilities even in summer, so take a picnic and water.

➕ 14H 🍴 None 🚤 Boat trips from Ciutadella and Cala en Bosc in summer

CALA BLANCA

This pretty pine-fringed cove, just 4km (2.5 miles) south of Ciutadella, has been blighted in recent years by excessive development. Once there was just a small beach nestling between low limestone cliffs; now it has been engulfed to such an extent that the beach is a mere speck on the map of the 'village'. The beach is overlooked by several restaurants, all competing to attract families with facilities ranging from swimming pools and water slides to games rooms and pool tables. At the back of the beach are the remains of a Bronze Age *naveta*.

➕ 2E 🍴 Several restaurants and bars (€€) 🚌 Buses from Ciutadella in summer

CALA EN BLANES

The coastline to the west of Ciutadella was once a succession of small beaches and pretty coves; now Cala en Blanes, along with its neighbours Cala en Bruc, Cala en Forcat and Cales Piques, have been swallowed up and merged into one continuous stretch of 'urbanization', based around the busy tourist complex of Los Delfines. This is as close as Menorca gets to the mass tourist developments of the Spanish *costas*, with signs in English and German, villas in fake local style, overcrowding in summer and a complete absence of life in winter. At the heart of the resort, **Aquapark** (➤ 70) is Menorca's first waterpark, with waterslides, soft play areas and crazy golf for the kids.

✚ 1D 🍴 Beach bars and restaurants (€–€€) 🚌 Buses from Ciutadella

Aquapark

☎ 971 38 87 05 🕔 May–Oct daily 10:30–6 💆 Expensive

CALA EN BOSC

Just 9km (5.5 miles) south of Ciutadella and easily reached on a fast road, Cala en Bosc has become one of Menorca's most fashionable resorts. Life revolves around the marina, built on the site of a drained wetland, and lined with smart restaurants and bars. Small boats can enter the marina through a narrow channel;

this is also a departure point for cruises to the more remote coves along the south coast. The neighbouring resort of Son Xoriguer, with its large twin beaches, is a centre for water sports, with schools offering windsurfing, water-skiing, scuba-diving and sailing. Both resorts are heavily developed and not for those seeking peace and quiet.

✚ 2F 🍴 Wide choice of beachside restaurants (€€) 🚌 Buses from Ciutadella in summer

CALA MORELL

Eight kilometres (5 miles) from Ciutadella on the otherwise deserted northeast coast, Cala Morell is best known for its remarkable collection of prehistoric caves. Dating from the late Bronze and early Iron Ages, and used both as burial caves and as dwellings, they feature circular chambers with central pillars plus windows, chimneys and raised sleeping areas. Some even have elaborately carved motifs on their facades. It is easy to get into most of the caves; if your appetite is whetted, finds from these caves are on display at the Museu de Menorca in Maó (➤ 87) and the Museu Municipal in Ciutadella (➤ 164–165).

There is a small beach here, reached by steps from the car parks at either end of the village, and there is good swimming and snorkelling from the rock platforms at the foot of the cliffs. The *urbanización* above the beach, a collection of Ibizan-style whitewashed villas, is one of the most exclusive in Menorca. As you wander around the prehistoric caves, you cannot help wondering whether the tourists of 3,000 years' time will be clambering over the ruins of these villas and speculating on early 21st-century life.

✚ 3B 🍴 Bars and restaurants in village (€€)

CALA SANTANDRÍA

This long, narrow creek, just 3km (2 miles) south of Ciutadella, would be pretty if it did not get so crowded. Along with its satellite cove Sa Caleta, it is the beach which Ciutadellans head for at weekends. There are several bars and restaurants, and all the usual facilities, including hire of pedal boats, umbrellas and loungers.

✚ 2D 🍴 Bars and restaurants (€€)
🚌 Buses from Ciutadella in summer

ERMITA DE SANT JOAN DE MISSA (GRAN)

This 15th-century Gothic church, brilliantly whitewashed and visible for miles around, is only used once a year – on the eve of the Festa de Sant Joan (➤ 24), when a horseback procession from Ciutadella rides out for a traditional Mass before returning to the city for the festivities. At most other times the church is locked, but if you're on your way to Cala en Turqueta (➤ 140) or

Cala Macarella (➤ 142–143) it's worth stopping to look at the small gabled bell-tower and the ivy branches across the arched facade.

✚ 3E 🕐 Mon 4–7 🍴 None
❓ Mass and procession on 23 Jun

NAVETA DES TUDONS

Best places to see, ➤ 44–45.

PUNTA NATI

Drive out here on a windy day – or take a bike – and you will see why Menorca is called an island of stones and wind. The 6km (4-mile) road to the island's northwestern tip has little to offer apart from endless vistas of a barren, rocky landscape punctuated by stepped *ponts*, the drystone sheep and cattle sheds which protect the livestock from the extremes of the weather and help clear the fields of unwanted stones. On the wind-buffeted headland, as ever, the lighthouse is off limits, but you can walk along the cliffs to a couple of deserted coves.

✚ 1B 🍴 None

S'HOSTAL

Menorca's most unusual tourist attraction is a disused sandstone quarry outside Ciutadella, which has been turned into a monument to the island's history and traditions of quarrying. Sandstone has been used for building since prehistoric times; soft and permeable, hence easy to extract, it turns hard when exposed to the air and is the perfect building material. Traditionally it was extracted by hammer and chisel; the few remaining quarries use circular saws which dig deep into the ground, creating vertical walls of white stone.

The quarry closed in 1994; it was bought up by Líthica and reopened the following year. You can walk around a 'labyrinth of orchards' in the old quarry, now turned into a garden, then descend to the giant white amphitheatre of the modern quarry, 30m (98ft) deep, where on weekdays workmen give displays of quarrying and at other times you stand in the eerie quiet of a sandstone cathedral. Ambitious plans for this site mean it now has a maze, a sculpture park, a visitor centre and a concert auditorium beneath the sheer white walls. An industrial wasteland has been creatively transformed into an unexpectedly special place.

🚌 3D 📧 2km (1.2 miles) from Ciutadella on Camí Vell de Maó ☎ 971 48 15 78 🕐 Daily 9:30–sunset in summer; free access in winter ♿ Inexpensive 🍴 None

SON CATLAR

Menorca's largest megalithic settlement is reached on the road from Ciutadella to Arenal de Son Saura. Built around 1800BC, it grew to its present size in Roman times and continued to be occupied right up to the Middle Ages. The most impressive feature here is the surrounding wall, some 900m (2,950ft) in circumference and built of massive stones – walls such as this one are often known as Cyclopean because of the belief that only giants could have built them. A doorway at the north side of the wall leads to a *taula* precinct, but the horizontal stone on top of the *taula* has fallen and collapsed. Son Catlar has helpful, multi-lingual information boards to guide you around

✚ 3E ⊙ Apr–Oct daily 9:30–sunset; free access in winter ⏹ None ✋ Inexpensive

HOTELS

CIUTADELLA

Esmeralda (€€)

Typical 1960s seaside hotel, beside the Passeig Marítim. Most rooms have sea-facing balconies. Swimming pool, tennis courts and a children's play area.

✉ Avinguda Sant Nicolau 171 ☎ 971 38 02 50; www.mac-hotels.com
🕐 May–Oct

Oasis (€)

Small, modest *hostal* near the ring road with nine rooms around a central courtyard.

✉ Carrer Sant Isidre 33 ☎ 971 38 21 97 🕐 Apr–Oct

Paris (€)

Simple rooms in an old-style Menorcan house on the edge of town, close to Cala des Degollador beach.

✉ Carretera Santandria 4 ☎ 971 38 16 22 🕐 Apr–Oct

Playa Grande (€€)

Small, modern hotel beside the beach at Cala des Degollador with expected facilities, plus balconies overlooking the start of the Passeig Marítim.

✉ Carrer Bisbe Juano 2 ☎ 971 48 08 64; www.grupoandria.com

Sant Ignasi (€€€)

Former 18th-century summer house turned into a rural hotel with lush gardens, a swimming pool and Anglo–Menorcan furniture.

✉ Carrer Cala Morell ☎ 971 38 55 75; www.santignasi.com 🕐 Jan–Nov

CALA EN BLANES

Almirante Farragut (€€)

This massive hotel (880 beds) dominates the small cove of Cala en Forcat. Facilities include swimming pool, tennis courts, mini-golf and bike rental.

✉ Cala en Forcat ☎ 971 38 80 00 🕐 May–Oct

CALA EN BOSC
Cala'n Bosch (€€)
Large hotel with rooms overlooking the sea and all the usual facilities, including half-board.

✉ Urbanización Cala en Bosc ☎ 971 38 70 00 🕐 May–Oct

La Quinta (€€€)
Five-star spa hotel in colonial-style buildings around a pool. Facilities include bike rental, golf practice area and health centre. A short walk from Son Xoriguer beach, and shuttle buses to Ciutadella.

✉ Avinguda Son Xoriguer ☎ 971 05 50 00; www.laquintamenorca.com
🕐 May–Oct

CALA MORELL
Biniatram (€€)
A 500-year-old farmhouse, with its own private chapel, on a working dairy. Tennis court and swimming pool.

✉ Carretera de Cala Morell ☎ 971 38 31 13; www.biniatram.com

RESTAURANTS

CIUTADELLA
Aurora (€)
Fishy *tapas* and fresh seafood on a lively square where the old town meets the new.

✉ Plaça Alfons III 3 ☎ 971 38 00 29 🕐 Lunch and dinner

Café Balear (€€€)
The perfect setting for lunch by the harbour; plenty of fresh shellfish plus steaks and *carpaccio* of veal.

✉ Passeig de Sant Joan 15 ☎ 971 38 00 05; www.cafe-balear.com
🕐 Lunch and dinner. Closed Sun in summer, Mon in winter

Ca'n Nito (€€)
Tapas bar on the edge of the Born with lots of fish dishes and charcoal-grilled steaks.

✉ Plaça des Born 11 ☎ 971 48 07 68 🕐 All day

Cas Ferrer (€€€)

An old blacksmith's forge now a tasteful terrace restaurant, offering a changing menu of modern Mediterranean dishes.

✉ Carrer Portal de Sa Font 16 ☎ 971 480784 🕙 Lunch and dinner, Tue–Sat

Casa Manolo (€€€)

Top-notch fresh seafood and lobster dishes beside the harbour walls.

✉ Marina 117–121 ☎ 971 38 00 03 🕙 Lunch and dinner

Club Náutico (€€)

Serious fish dishes in the yacht club restaurant overlooking the port.

✉ Camí Baix, beneath Passeig Marítim ☎ 971 38 27 73; www.cnciutadella.com 🕙 Lunch and dinner

El Horno (€€)

Intimate basement French restaurant near the Plaça des Born.

✉ Carrer des Forn 12 ☎ 971 38 07 67 🕙 Apr–Oct dinner only

Es Moll (€€)

On the far side of the harbour from the rows of identical fish restaurants, offering a simpler lunchtime menu, including pizzas.

✉ Moll Commercial ☎ 971 480813 🕙 Lunch and dinner

La Guitarra (€€)

Classic Menorcan dishes – duck, roast lamb, snails – served in an atmospheric cellar.

✉ Carrer Nostra Senyora dels Dolors 1 ☎ 971 38 13 55 🕙 Closed Sun

La Payesa (€€)

A large choice of seafood dishes including three different *paellas*, plus international offerings and a children's menu.

✉ Port of Ciutadella ☎ 971 38 00 21 🕙 Lunch and dinner

Pa Amb Oli (€€)

The name means 'bread and oil', a popular local snack served with platters of sausages, ham, grilled vegetables or grilled meat in this busy restaurant close to Plaça des Born.

✉ Carrer Nou de Juliol 4 ☎ 971 38 36 19 🕓 Lunch and dinner, Mon–Sat

Restaurant d'Es Port (€€)

Fresh fish, seafood and grilled meats. The main restaurant has lobster and fish from its own boat.

✉ Port de Ciutadella ☎ 971 48 00 22 🕓 Lunch and dinner

Roma (€€)

The speciality here is pizza cooked in a wood-fired oven. Also Italian meat and fish dishes and fresh pasta.

✉ Carrer Pere d'Alcántara 18 ☎ 971 38 47 18; www.cafe-balear.com
🕓 Closed Sun lunch

Sa Figuera (€€)

Great grilled steaks, seafood dishes and *caldereta de langosta*.

✉ Port de Ciutadella ☎ 971 38 21 12 🕓 Lunch and dinner

CALA BLANCA
Es Caliu (€€)

A large and busy restaurant specializing in mouthwatering charcoal-grilled meats.

✉ Carretera Ciutadella–Cala en Bosc ☎ 971 38 01 65 🕓 Lunch and dinner daily in summer, weekends only in winter

CALA EN BOSC
Aquarium (€€€)

Fresh fish and seafood from Menorca and Galicia – crayfish, prawns, turbot in *cava* – at this top-notch harbourside restaurant.

✉ El Lago ☎ 971 38 74 42 🕓 May–Oct lunch and dinner daily

Café Balear (€€)

Specializes in seafood, with dishes ranging from plain grilled lobster to angler fish in almond sauce.

✉ El Lago ☎ 608 74 48 16; www.cafe-balear.com 🕓 Lunch and dinner daily in summer

Ca N'Anglada (€€)

Steaks, seafood and creative Mediterranean cuisine – a cut above the other places around the marina.

✉ El Lago ☎ 971 38 14 02 🕐 Lunch and dinner, Tue–Sun

SHOPPING

FOOD AND DRINK
Miguel Bagur

Pastry shop specializing in *ensaimadas* and delicious homemade biscuits.

✉ Carrer JM Quadrado 8 (Ses Voltes), Ciutadella ☎ 971 38 06 40

Ses Industries

Wines, liqueurs and cheese in olive oil in this Aladdin's cave near the cathedral.

✉ Carrer Santa Clara 7, Ciutadella ☎ 971 38 28 82

JEWELLERY
Carles

Old-fashioned jewellers' shop in the heart of the old city.

✉ Carrer Santa Clara 16, Ciutadella ☎ 971 38 07 34

Joies

This smart jewellery shop is in the pedestrian part of town.

✉ Carrer de Maó 6, Ciutadella ☎ 971 38 33 11

Joyería Anglada

Jewellery, silver, gold and Majórica pearls under the arches in Ses Voltes.

✉ Carrer JM Quadrado 23 (Ses Voltes), Ciutadella ☎ 971 38 15 48

LEATHER AND FASHION
Blau Mari

This fashionable shop in the vaults of the Palau Salord has a wide range of shoes, espadrilles, leather articles and colourful T-shirts.

✉ Carrer Major del Born 11, Ciutadella ☎ 971 48 10 95

Ca Sa Pollaca
Has been selling handmade leather shoes and sandals since 1897; tgreat selection of *abarcas* (rubber-soled sandals) for children.

✉ Carrer JM Quadrado 10 (Ses Voltes), Ciutadella ☎ 971 38 22 23

Looky
High-quality, locally made boots and shoes, as well as accessories such as belts and handbags from this well-established brand.

✉ Gustavo Más 16–18, Ciutadella ☎ 971 38 16 12; www.looky.es

Patricia
The largest branch of Patricia's empire is on the road out of town. Also shops in Carrer Seminari and on the harbour steps.

✉ Carretera Cala Santandría, Ciutadella ☎ 971 38 50 56

ENTERTAINMENT

BARS AND CLUBS
Bar Es Moli
This bar in the windmill in the centre of town tends to attract a young and often noisy crowd. Open until 1am or later.

✉ Cami de Mao 1, Ciutadella ☎ No telephone 🕒 Daily 11am–late

La Margarete
A stylish bar set around an attractive interior patio where Ciutadella's locals hang out.

✉ Carrer de Sant Joan, Ciutadella 🕒 Fri and Sat nights

Jazzbah
Cool, late-night jazz bar behind the harbour. Live music most weekends.

✉ Plaça de Sant Joan 3 ☎ 971 48 29 53 🕒 Jun–Sep daily 11pm–6am, weekends only in winter

DISCO
Lateral
The old warehouses around the Plaça de Sant Joan (the open space behind the marina) are home to numerous clubs and discos,

which get busy around midnight and continue into the small hours. This is probaby the best known. Just choose the music and the decor that suits your style – they change from year to year.

✉ Plaça de Sant Joan 9, Ciutadella ☎ 971 38 53 28

THEATRE
Teatre Municipal des Born
The city's theatre puts on concerts and performances in a 19th-century neoclassical building in a corner of the Born.

✉ Plaça des Born, Ciutdella ☎ 971 38 49 13

SPORT

BOAT TRIPS
Rutas Marítimas de la Cruz
Pack your swimwear for a day-long trip from Ciutadella, including lunch. There is a bar on board and ice creams are available.

✉ Muelle Comercial de Ciutadella ☎ 971 35 07 78;
www.rutasmaritimasdelacruz.com

DIVING SCHOOLS
Dive Cala Blanca
Everything for the holidaying diver of any standard.

✉ Avinguda Cala Blanca, Cala Blanca ☎ 617 65 69 06;
www.divecalablanca.com

HORSERACING
Hipódromo de Ciutadella
Trotting races held on Sunday, April to December, at 6pm.

✉ Torre del Ram, Cala en Blanes ☎ 971 38 80 38

WATER SPORTS
Surf'n'Sail Menorca
Windsurfing, sailing and water-skiing with modern equipment. Motor boats also available for rent.

✉ Platja Son Xoriguer, Cala en Bosc ☎ 971 38 71 05;
www.surfsailmenorca.com

Sight Locator Index

This index relates to the maps on the covers. We have given map references to the main sights of interest in the book. Grid references in italics indicate sights featured on the town plans. Some sights within towns may not be plotted on the maps.

Ajuntament (Ayuntamiento) *Maó 3c*
Alaior **20H**
Arenal d'en Castell **10C**
Arenal (Platges) de Son Saura **14H**
Ateneu *Maó 2c*
Barranc d'Algendar (Algendar Gorge) **5E**
Binibeca (Binibèquer) Vell **22L**
Binimel-là **7B**
Binisues (Binissuès) **5D**
Cala Blanca **2E**
Cala d'Alcaufar **23L**
Cala d'Algaiarens **4B**
Cala de Sant Esteve **24K**
Cala de Santa Galdana **15H**
Cala del Pilar **5B**
Cala en Blanes **1D**
Cala en Bosc **2F**
Cala en Porter **19K**
Cala en Turqueta **14H**
Cala Escorxada **16H**
Cala Figuera *Maó 8d*
Cala Macarella **15H**
Cala Mesquida **23J**
Cala Mitjana **15H**
Cala Morell **3B**
Cala Pregonda **7B**
Cala Presili **12D**
Cala Santandría **2D**
Cala Tirant **8B**
Cala Trebalúger **16H**
Cales Coves **20K**
Cap de Cavallería **8A**
Cap de Favàritx **12D**
Ciutadella (Ciudadela) **2D**
Collecció Hernández Mora *Maó 4c*
Cova des Coloms **17H**
Ermita de Sant Joan de Missa (Gran) **3E**
Es Castell **23K**
Es Mercadal **8D**
Es Migjorn Gran **17H**
Església del Carme *Maó 4c*

Ferreries **6D**
Fornells **9B**
Fort Sant Felip **23K**
Fortalesa de la Mola **24K**
Maó (Mahón) **23K**
Monte Toro **9D**
Museu de Menorca *Maó 2b*
Na Macaret **11C**
Naveta des Tudons **3D**
Plaça des Born, Ciutadella **2D**
Plaça de S'Esplanada *Maó 1d*
Port d'Addaia **11D**
Port de Maó (Maó Harbour) *Maó 4b*
Punta Nati **1B**
Punta Prima **23M**
Rafal Rubí **21J**
Sa Torreta **12E**
S'Albufera d'Es Grau **12E**
Sant Adeodat **17J**
Sant Agustí Vell **17H**
Sant Climent (San Clemente) **21K**
Sant Lluís (San Luio) **22L**
Sant Tomàs **17J**
Santa Agueda **6C**
Santa Maria *Maó 3c*
Shangri-La **22H**
S'Hostal **3D**
So Na Caçana (Casana) **20K**
Son Bou **18J**
Son Catlar **3E**
Son Parc **10C**
Talatí de Dalt **21J**
Teatre Principal *Maó 3c*
Torelló **21K**
Torralba d'en Salort **20J**
Torre d'en Gaumés **19J**
Torre Llafuda **4D**
Torre Llisà Vell **20J**
Torre Trencada **4D**
Trepucó **23K**
Xoriguer *Maó 2b*

Index

Acknowledgements

The Automobile Association would like to thank the following photographers, companies and picture libraries for their assistance in the preparation of this book.

Abbreviations for the picture credits are as follows: (t) top; (b) bottom; (c) centre; (l) left; (r) right; (AA) AA World Travel Library

6/7 Port d'Addaia, AA/J A Tims; **8/9** Cove near Cala Macarelleta, AA/J A Tims; **10/11** Cala Pregonda AA/J A Tims; **10c** Arenal d'en Castell, AA/J A Tims; **10bl** Cales Fonts, AA/J A Tims; **10br** Cala Macarella, AA/J A Tims; **11c** Pont de Sant Roc, AA/J A Tims; **11b** Pollenca, AA/P Baker; **12t** Spanish Restaurant, AA/M Chaplow; **12b** Meal, AA/K Paterson; **12/13** Placa Nova, AA/J A Tims; **13t** Traditional meal, AA/J A Tims; **14t** Alaior, cheese shop, AA/J A Tims; **14b** Cheese, Alaior, AA/J A Tims; **15c** Cocktails, AA/R Victor; **15b** Xoriguer gin, AA/J A Tims; **16c** Cathedral, Cuitadella, AA/J A Tims; **16b** Trotting track, Mao, AA/J A Tims; **16/17** Platja des Son Bou, AA/J A Tims; **17** Cala Blanca, AA/J A Tims; **18t** Cala Coves, AA/J A Tims; **18b** Monte Toro, AA/J A Tims; **19** Cuitadella, AA/J A Tims; **20** Port De Pollenca, AA/P Baker; **24/25** Flora, AA/K Paterson; **27** Mao, harbour, AA/J A Tims; **28/29** Fornells, AA/J A Tims; **30** Postbox, AA/P Baker; **31** Fornells, AA/J A Tims; **32** Shopping, AA/C Sawyer; **34/35** Mao, AA/J A Tims; **36** Barranc d'Algendar, AA/J A Tims; **36/37** Barranc d'Algendar, shrine, AA/J A Tims; **38** Cala Pregonda, AA/J A Tims; **38/39** Beach, Cala Pregonda, AA/J A Tims; **40/41** Fornells, AA/J A Tims; **41** Fornells, Building detail, AA/J A Tims; **42c** Monte Toro, AA/J A Tims; **42b** View from Monte Toro, AA/J A Tims; **43** Statue, Monte Toro, AA/J A Tims; **44/45** Naveta des Tudons, AA/J A Tims; **46t** Placa d'es Born, Cuitadella, AA/J A Tims; **46/47** Placa d'es Born, Cuitadella. AA/J A Tims; **47** Placa d'es Born, Cuitdella, AA/J A Tims; **48** Mao harbour, AA/J A Tims; **48/49** Mao harbour, AA/J A Tims; **50/51** S'Albufera, AA/J A Tims; **52/53** Platja des Son Bou, AA/J A Tims; **53** Platja des Son Bou, AA/J A Tims; **54** Torre d'en Guames, AA/J A Tims; **54/55** Torre d'en Gaumes. AA/J A Tims; **56/57** Cala Pregonda, AA/J A Tims; **58/59** Cuitadella, AA/J A Tims; **60/61** Ciutadella old town, AA/J A Tims; **62/63** Colonia de Sant Jordi, AA/P Baker; **64/65** Punta Prima, AA/J A Tims; **66/67** Cala Macarelleta, AA/J A Tims; **68/69** Cap de Cavalleria, AA/J A Tims; **71** Alaior, AA/J A Tims; **72/73** Binibeca Vell, AA/J A Tims; **73** Punta Prima, AA/J A Tims; **75** Cala Morell, AA/J A Tims; **76/77** Platje de Son Bou, AA/J A Tims; **78/79** Cathedral, Cuitadella, AA/J A Tims; **81** Cala d'Alcaufar, AA/J A Tims; **83** Town Hall, Mao, AA/J A Tims; **84/85** Cala Figuera, AA/J A Tims; **86** Eglesia del Carme, AA/J A Tims; **87t** Museu Municipal de Menorca, AA/J A Tims; **87b** Museu Municipal de Menorca, AA/J A Tims; **90/91** Place des S'Esplanada, Mao, AA/J A Tims; **91** Church of Santa Maria, Mao, AA/J A Tims; **92** Binibeca Vell, AA/J A Tims; **93** Binibeca Vell, AA/J A Tims; **94** Cala d'Alcaufar, AA/J A Tims; **94/95** Cala de Sant Esteve, AA/J A Tims; **95** Cala Mesquida, AA/J A Tims; **96** Placa de S'Esplanada, AA/J A Tims; **96/97** Fort Sant Felip, AA/J A Tims; **98/99** Cales Fonts, AA/J A Tims; **100/101** Punta Prima, AA/J A Tims; **101** Moli de Dalt, AA/J A Tims; **102t** Talatide Dalt, AA/J A Tims; **102b** Es Fornas de Torellu, AA/J A Tims; **103** Trepuco, monuments, AA/J A Tims; **115** Torralba d'en Salord, AA/J A Tims; **116** Santa Eulalia, Alaior, AA/J A Tims; **116/117** Arenal d'en Castell, AA/J A Tims; **118** Cove d'En Xoroi, AA/J A Tims; **120** Cales Coves, AA/J A Tims; **120/121** Cales Coves, AA/J A Tims; **121** Cales Coves, AA/J A Tims; **122t** Cap Cavalleria, AA/J A Tims; **122b** Cap de Favaritx, AA/J A Tims; **123** Carrer Major, AA/J A Tims; **124/125** Na Macaret, AA/J A Tims; **125** Port d'Addala, AA/J A Tims; **126/127** Shangri-La Village, AA/J A Tims; **127** S'Albufera des Grau, AA/J A Tims; **128/129** S'Albufera des Grau, AA/J A Tims; **129** Sa Torreta, AA/J A Tims; **130/131** Torralba d'en Salord, AA/J A Tims; **132** Torre Llisa Vell, AA/J A Tims; **137** Barranc d'Algendar, AA/J A Tims; **138** Binimel-la, AA/J A Tims; **138/139** Binisues, AA/J A Tims; **139** Binisues, AA/J A Tims; **140** Cala del Pilar, AA/J A Tim; **140/141** Cala En Turqueta, AA/J A Tims; **142/143** Cala Macarella, AA/J A Tims; **143** Cala Mitjana, AA/J A Tims; **144** Cala Santa Galdana, AA/J A Tims; **144/145** Cala Santa Galdana, AA/J A Tims; **146** Cova des Coloms, AA/J A Tims; **147c** Es Migjorn Gran, AA/J A Tims; **147b** Es Migjorn Gran, AA/J A Tims; **148/149** Ferreries, AA/J A Tims; **149** Sant Adeodato, AA/J A Tims; **150** Moli de Dalt windmill, AA/J A Tims; **150/151** Son Mercer de Baix, AA/J A Tims; **152/153** Puig de Santa Agueda, AA/J A Tims; **159** Ermita de Sant Joan de Missa, AA/J A Tims; **161** Cuitadella, AA/J A Tims; **162** Cathedral, Cuitadella, AA/J A Tims; **164/165** Museu Municipal de Menorca, AA/J A Tims; **166/167** Museu Municipal de Menorca, AA/J A Tims; **168/169** Palau Salord, AA/J A Tims; **168** Palau Salord, AA/J A Tims; **170** Cuitadella, statue, AA/J A Tims; **171** Cami d'en Kane, AA/J A Tims; **172t** Convent de Santa Clara, AA/J A Tims; **172c** Convent de Santa Clara, Cuitadella, AA/J A Tims; **173** Arenal de Son Saura, AA/J A Tims; **174** Cala en Bosc, AA/J A Tims; **175** Cala Morell, AA/J A Tims; **176/177t** Santandrai, AA/J A Tims; **176** Church of Sant Joan de Missa, AA/J A Tims; **176/177b** Punta Nati, AA/J A Tims; **178/179** S'Hostal, AA/J A Tims; **179** Son Catlar, AA/J A Tims

Every effort has been made to trace the copyright holders, and we apologise in advance for any accidental errors. We would be happy to apply the corrections in the following edition of this publication.

Dear Reader

Your comments, opinions and recommendations are very important to us. Please help us to improve our travel guides by taking a few minutes to complete this simple questionnaire.

You do not need a stamp (unless posted outside the UK). If you do not want to cut this page from your guide, then photocopy it or write your answers on a plain sheet of paper

Send to: **The Editor, AA World Travel Guides,**
FREEPOST SCE 4598, Basingstoke RG21 4GY.

Your recommendations...

We always encourage readers' recommendations for restaurants, nightlife or shopping – if your recommendation is used in the next edition of the guide, we will send you a **FREE AA Guide** of your choice from this series. Please state below the establishment name, location and your reasons for recommending it.

_____

_____

_____

_____

_____

Please send me **AA Guide** _____

About this guide...

Which title did you buy?

AA _____

Where did you buy it? _____

When? m m / y y

Why did you choose this guide? _____

_____

_____

_____

Did this guide meet your expectations?

Exceeded ☐   Met all ☐   Met most ☐   Fell below ☐

Were there any aspects of this guide that you particularly liked? _____

_____

_____

continued on next page...

Is there anything we could have done better? _____
_____
_____
_____

About you...
Name (*Mr/Mrs/Ms*) _____
Address _____
_____
_____ Postcode _____

Daytime tel nos _____
Email _____

Please only give us your mobile phone number or email if you wish to hear from us about other products and services from the AA and partners by text or mms, or email.

Which age group are you in?
Under 25 ☐ 25–34 ☐ 35–44 ☐ 45–54 ☐ 55–64 ☐ 65+ ☐

How many trips do you make a year?
Less than one ☐ One ☐ Two ☐ Three or more ☐

Are you an AA member? Yes ☐ No ☐

About your trip...
When did you book? m m / y y   When did you travel? m m / y y

How long did you stay? ___._____

Was it for business or leisure? _____

Did you buy any other travel guides for your trip? _____

If yes, which ones? _____
_____
_____

Thank you for taking the time to complete this questionnaire. Please send it to us as soon as possible, and remember, you do not need a stamp (*unless posted outside the UK*).

AA Travel Insurance call 0800 072 4168 or visit www.theAA.com

---